JOURNEY TO IMPACT

A PRACTICAL GUIDE TO PURPOSE-DRIVEN INVESTING

ED GILLENTINE

Published by Innovo Publishing, LLC
www.innovopublishing.com
1-888-546-2111

Providing Full-Service Publishing Services for Christian Authors,
Artists & Ministries:
Books, eBooks, Audiobooks, Music, Film & Courses

JOURNEY TO IMPACT:
*A Practical Guide to
Purpose-Driven Investing*

ISBN: 978-1-61314-546-3

Cover Design & Interior Layout: Innovo Publishing, LLC

Printed in the United States of America
U.S. Printing History
First Edition: 2019

ENDORSEMENTS

"Ed Gillentine masterfully invites the reader alongside his honest, introspective journey to impact that both inspires and challenges the mind, soul, and wallet to focus on sustainable, yet practical solutions that are aligned with the needs of the communities we want to serve."
——**Dr. Floyd Tyler, President & Chief Investment Officer, Preserver Partners; Tri-State Bank Board of Directors**

"This book needed to be written, and fortunately it was written by a man that has lived this journey and can truly guide the readers through their own journey to impact. Ed is a bright, articulate man—the title says so much by using two of the most powerful words in the English language: *impact* and *purpose*. This book is truly a guide. If you are interested in making an impact with a purpose, you will wear this book out with your underlining and margin notes."
——**Ken Edmundson, CEO, The Edmundson Group; Author of *ShortTrack CEO* and *Teamwork*; Founder of the ShortTrack Business Management System**

"An outstanding work on impact investing, and a must read for anyone wanting to make a difference. This book will show you how to deploy your resources for the long-term good of others in a way that is best suited to your gifts and talents."
——**Lieutenant Colonel Harry Jones, PhD Philosophy, Assistant Professor of Philosophy, United States Military Academy**

"Journey to Impact is a practical and powerful guide for those who seek to harness their gifts in service to the world. Ed writes from experience, shares from the heart, and offers us clear frameworks and guideposts as we navigate the challenging process of discovering our own personal calling. Asking, *What am I to do?* can be an overwhelming question to answer, but with the help of this book, we can, with a little more courage and clarity, begin to chart our own paths toward making a difference."
—David Ellis, CEO, Flow Equity; Impact Investor

"Life is short. What matters is not how long we live but what impact we make during the time we are given. *Journey to Impact* is practical and concise, and it has challenged me to think about purpose-driven impact from a new and fresh perspective. This is a must-read book! Please, join the journey!"
—Andinet Meaza, Chief Operating Officer, Highland Harvesters Fruit & Agriculture, PLC, Addis Ababa, Ethiopia

"It never ceases to amaze me how many American businessmen, accomplished in their careers stateside and self-confident in their instincts and business savvy, go to Africa to replicate their business successes there. Then they fail, and fail spectacularly, having no idea what all went wrong. Ed Gillentine is one of the few I've met who has unlocked Africa's entrepreneurial secrets. If you are going to Africa to set up a for-profit (or non-profit, for that matter), you'd be smart to take Ed along as your guide. Ed knows the territory. He understands the obstacles. He anticipates the pitfalls. Ed sees with clarity what apparently is nearly invisible to everyone else."
—David Caldwell, CEO, Dalen Products; Impact Investor

"Theory in impact investing is everywhere, particularly for wealthy people and foundations. Practical wisdom for those of us with more modest means is harder to find. Ed Gillentine has created a great resource, based on his own experience in Memphis and in Ethiopia. The book will greatly improve your chances of success, as you clarify your own social impact goals and set out, against all odds, to achieve them. Ed leads by doing and invites you to do the same."
—**Phil Cubeta, "Sallie B. and William B. Wallace Chair in Philanthropy," CAP Program Director, American College**

"Living a life intended for impact requires a deliberate effort to understand what type of impact you want to make in your community, or if you are thinking bigger, in the world. *Journey to Impact* is full of practical principles and steps that help align your passions, experiences, and resources to maximize a purpose-driven impact that is unique to you and your family."
—**Lauren Young, Founder, Sweet LaLa's Bakery; Baptist Memorial Healthcare Foundation Board of Directors; Christian Community Foundation Board of Directors; St. George's Independent School Board of Directors**

"I've been a close friend of Ed's for over a decade now, and over that time, he has subtly encouraged me to think bigger and better about how I can use my resources to the highest degree of impact. If you have any desire to be generous but are not sure how to use your unique gifts or resources (whatever they are) to allow others a chance to flourish, then read this book. It is an excellent and practical compilation of Ed's thoughts, experiences, and passions put into action."
—**John Ozier, President, UWT Logistics; Managing Partner, Highland Harvesters, LLC; Impact Investor**

"In sports, we know what the goal is—to win the game against our opponent—and we often use *impact* to tackle, steal, or block to keep the other side from scoring. Ed Gillentine's book, *Journey to Impact*, is full of wisdom that comes from his work in Memphis, TN, as well as dozens of overseas mission trips. Ed has found a passion for Ethiopia in particular and now leads us through the critical 'planning stages' that have allowed him to provide a very effective winning process in serving hundreds both overseas and at home. Ed teaches us how to create our own purpose-driven concept that can be highly successful wherever we choose to serve."

**—Kyle Rote, Jr., U.S. Soccer Hall of Fame;
Popular Christian Speaker; Board of Directors, FCA**

"*Journey to Impact* provides a brilliant and vivid roadmap to blessing others and creating a legacy that is God-pleasing and fulfills your personal purpose. If you are committed to making a difference for eternity but are not sure how, this book is a must read."

**—Kevin W. Westbrook, PhD Professor of Marketing,
McAfee School of Business, Union University**

"Impact is something we are all looking to make. We want to impact our bank accounts with big deposits, our children with wise parenting, our bodies with food and exercise—and the list goes on. Many of us also long to impact those outside our immediate sphere of influence. You've probably heard it said, 'I want to change the world.' Well, changing the world may be quite a feat, but, we all can impact a life, maybe even many lives, when we are willing to make sacrifices for others. Ed Gillentine helps us see how our experiences, skills, innate gifts, and placement in this world combine to point us towards our unique opportunity for impact. If you are ready to see how you can impact others, maybe even many others, this book is for you."

—Joe Bridges, Founder of The Forsaken Children

To Sosie:
Only God knows the lives you've impacted along your journey.

CONTENTS

ACKNOWLEDGMENTS

One does not write a book of this sort without an awful lot of help, encouragement, and critique. And that is certainly true of *Journey to Impact*. I can't remember the last time I had an original thought or idea! So my journey has been learning from others (some of whom don't even realize it!). There is no way to mention everyone, but there are some that I simply can't help but mention.

Joe and Karyn Bridges: God used you guys to bring Liz and I (and our hearts) to Ethiopia. You've shaped our view of at-risk children like no one else. You were passionate about sustainability before anyone else was talking about it. You helped pour our Impact foundation!

Jonathan Bridges: Highland Harvesters (HH) was born sitting on your back porch in Chencha, sucking on sugar cane (you have the scar to prove it!). HH has been one of the main classrooms for my journey. No words can express how grateful I am for your friendship. Thanks for being patient as I continue to try to learn the Ethiopian culture. Thanks most of all for being a man I can trust with my life (which I have done at least a couple of times already!).

John Ozier: Jesus and the journey has made us brothers. Mekele, Sodo, Chencha, Bele, and all the rest. Shintobets, tibs, sacrificial goats, and more coffee than we could have ever imagined. There is no Highland Harvesters without you. I don't think my journey would have ever happened with you.

Andinet Meaza: Benney's second birthday party was a game-changer! Who would have thought the godfather of apples in Ethiopia was ready for us to find him? You are my brother. There is no way to calculate the lives you have impacted, not only in Ethiopia but around the world.

ACKNOWLEDGMENTS

David Caldwell: Thanks for letting me observe, advise, and learn from your experiences. Not everyone has the opportunity to test drive impact theories like you have allowed me to do.

David Ellis and Joe Shields: Thanks for letting me observe, ask questions, and learn from both your successes and mistakes. And special thanks for educating me about chickens. I never knew how violent they were until I visited Mekele!

Tom Phillips: To this day I'm amazed that you took so much time to answer questions and mentor me over the years. And thank you for patiently and graciously talking me out of chickens!

Lauren Young: Your journey inspires me. Thanks for the encouragement and the feedback. I'm honored to call you and Tommy my friends.

Harry Jones: Thanks for all your help during the editing process. I've always wanted to process information as fast and as well as you. But, since I can't, it's nice to know you can do it for me! No one will ever know how much you added to this book by challenging me to keep rewriting until I got it right (or at least closer to right!). Thanks!

Mike Harris: You helped me break my paradigm. The miracle of the DALF is your idea.

Nega Meaza, OCDA staff, and all the kids at the Drop-In Center in 2009: You showed me that reality could be trumped by hope.

Alemayu: Your story keeps me going.

Greg Sperry: You're an impact genius! Thanks for being patient with me.

Bob Collins and Chok-Pin Foo: I learned more about impact in one afternoon with you guys than in ten years trying to figure it out on my own!

The Highland Harvesters Team—TJ, Andu, JF, Munita, Meron, Gedu, Berahan, and all the rest. You are all amazing!

Chris Hill, Scott Seese, Alan Barnhart, Ken Edmundson, Floyd Tyler, Phil Cubeta, Steve Nash, Justin Miller, Huff Peeler, Don Simmons, Kyle Rote, Jr., Kevin Westbrook, and Jason Fisher: Thanks.

Dr. Rick Jensen: You were the impetus for *Journey to Impact*. Thanks for planting the seed and for pushing me to take the next step.

The FOG Boys: Thanks for the encouragement!

My colleagues at the Gillentine Group—Stephen Chandler, Henry Greinke, Dorothy Westmoreland: You read and edited multiple drafts and advised on content. You shouldered the load at the office to allow me time to think and write. Thanks for everything. Especially the encouragement!

Mom and Dad: Thanks for the first lawnmower. Sometimes I think I should repay you, but then I think about ten years of hard labor under the auspices of "building a work ethic," and I think I'm good!

Jamie: Thanks for the G.I. Joes!

Mullin, Maddie, and Gabe: Thanks for your patience. Thanks for letting me travel so much. Most of all, thanks for being a reflection of what it means to journey toward impact.

Liz: Words can't express what you mean to me. Without you, there is no journey. You've helped me process information, dreams, emotions, successes, and failures. You've called me out when necessary. You let me think out loud, even when it makes no sense. Your wisdom has shaped my worldview more than any other. You have given most along this journey. Here's to many more miles with you!

FOREWORD

In the fall of 2017, I was challenged to write a book about what I had learned along my own personal *journey to impact*. I ignored the challenge for about six months. But sometime in the spring of 2018, I felt like it was a challenge I needed to accept. Candidly, I never thought it would make it through the vetting and critiques of the publishing process. But I thought that at the very least, it would help me to synopsize what I had learned so that I could more effectively continue along my own personal, lifelong journey to impact.

Over the year or so that it took to complete the project, I experienced a lot of ups and downs. Some days it seemed as though I could write forever in a way that was coherent, logical, and practical. Other days, it seemed as though I couldn't write a single sentence that made any sense at all. There were times when writing about my experiences reminded me of how far I had come along the journey and how much positive impact had been made. But there were just as many times that my writing reminded me of colossal failures and unintentional pain that I had caused.

For me, just as it has been along my own personal *journey to impact*, the benefit of writing this book has been in the process. Writing and rewriting, clarifying and re-clarifying, editing and re-editing, have all taught me more about myself than I could have ever imagined.

But now it's done. When I took my hands off and passed it off to the publisher, it was one of the hardest things I have ever done. Because I knew it wasn't perfect. I knew I would always think of ways to improve. Yet I knew I had to let go. The final chapter in the *Journey to Impact* is entitled "Get Off the Bench!" And I knew that after all the planning and editing and writing, it was time for me to take my own medicine and "get off the bench!"

When you finish this book, my prayer is that at least three things will have happened:

1. You will embrace your unique purpose for being on this planet for the days you have been given.

2. You will carefully and thoughtfully build a framework and a strategy for your unique impact.

3. You will take action to execute intentional, purpose-driven impact.

Thanks for taking the time to read this book. I hope to see you along the way as we all *journey to impact*.

Godspeed,

Ed Gillentine

Memphis, TN

CHAPTER 1

MY JOURNEY

You can spend your life any way you want, but you'll only spend it once. (Benjamin Franklin)

In March of 2011, I stood on the balcony of a guest house in Addis Ababa, Ethiopia. It had been a long day working in a make-shift medical and dental clinic to serve the at-risk children in one of the poorest neighborhoods in the city. Darkness had fallen over the city, and from my vantage point, I could see millions of twinkling lights sparkling like candles. The capital city of Ethiopia is a city that, by some estimates, is home to over six million people, the vast majority of whom were trapped in a crushing cycle of generational poverty with no way of escape. It was at that moment that the two questions that would jumpstart my *journey to impact* became clear.

1. In a world of such vast resources juxtaposed to such overwhelming need, why are we having so little impact on the issues that matter most to humanity?

2. Why, in many cases, do our well-intentioned attempts to alleviate need cause so much harm?

These two questions have driven my *journey to impact* over the past decade. And this book is a synopsis of some of the things I have learned and observed. As I travel the globe and speak to individuals as well as groups about the subject of impact, I have realized that we are all asking similar questions—questions about some of the most painful and difficult issues of our time. Yet no matter how tangled, nuanced, and twisted the journey might be, we must pursue the answers. Because the issues affect millions of people around the globe in very real, tangible, and personal ways.

Hopefully you will be able to learn from the mistakes I and others have made. And throughout the process, you will glean some principles on which you can build your own uniquely personal framework of impact. A framework that will catapult you to significant, catalytic, and generational impact.

From the outset, it is probably just as important to say what this book is *not* about as it is to communicate what it *is* about. For starters, it is not about triggering feelings of guilt. Not only is that an overused and crude attempt to enjoin action, it's simply ineffective. This book is not about shaming the wealthy about second homes, nice vacations, and private schools. I have never found wealth and how it is allocated to be the primary problem among those who want to have impact.

> *Good intentions do not necessarily lead to good results.*

Nor is this a book about criticizing the passion and good intentions with which many people and organizations have attempted to answer these great questions over the years. I rarely meet people who don't have good intentions. But good intentions do not necessarily lead to good results.

Simply put, this is a book about impact. It's about significant, strategic, and positive impact that is unique to you. And it's about how you can have it.

Truth be told, my *journey to impact* began many years before that night in Addis Ababa, Ethiopia, in March of 2011. It actually began as a young boy.

I've always had a fascination with wealth. Not only its accumulation but also its purpose and its impact. Somewhere along the way I read a quote attributed to Confucius:

Money is like fire. It's an excellent tool but a terrible master.

And I suppose that even as I talked my brother into buying the G.I. Joes or Lego sets that I wanted (so I wouldn't have to spend my own money), I sensed that wealth had power to do great good as well as great harm.

As a young child, two things were ingrained in me relative to wealth. First, that work, and hard work I should add, is a good, healthy, and God-honoring thing. And through work, one *earned* a living. I can't tell you how many times I heard the ancient scripture, "If any should not work, neither shall he eat" (2 Thes 3:10 KJV). So I learned that working hard should lead to earning a livelihood, which in our culture today usually equals money.

As soon as I could talk my dad into letting me use the lawnmower, I began asking the neighbors if I could mow their grass. At twenty dollars for a yard that took approximately one hour to mow, I thought I was on track to be a millionaire by the time I was in college! And when I added in premium services such as edging, weed trimming, and bagging the grass, I could make even more money!

The second thing I learned as a young boy was that I had a responsibility to give to charity a portion of the wealth that I earned. As far back as I can remember, that was non-negotiable. It wasn't really debated or discussed much. It just was. And so as soon as I collected the very first twenty dollars I earned from mowing the next door neighbor's yard, I set aside ten percent to give to my church. If you have grown up in or around religion, you will be familiar with the idea of a tithe. If you didn't, don't worry. The amount doesn't really matter. The point is that we should all be generous with the financial resources with which we have been entrusted, and those resources are to be used to help others.

So along with learning that working hard should lead to earning money, I learned that earning money created an opportunity for generosity. And I learned that money was a tool, not the purpose. It's a tool to be used for good and to do good.

Without even realizing it, my initial trajectory as it relates to impact was being set as a young child. The basic framework through which I view wealth to this very day was in large part settled before I was twelve years old.

In addition to the foundation laid by my parents, teachers, pastors, and friends, there were two events that had major repercussions on my *journey to impact*. They weren't earth-shattering. They weren't accompanied by fireworks or miracles. I didn't even realize their significance for days or weeks afterward. Probably not even for years. But nonetheless, they profoundly affected my *journey to impact*.

The first happened while I was in high school. My father was one of the ministers at our local church, and one of his responsibilities was to visit people who were in the hospital. On one particular afternoon, I had a baseball game and he was my ride. He had to make a stop at the hospital to visit a sick church member on the way to the game, so I joined him.

I had never met this particular family before, but they graciously invited me into the hospital room along with my dad to visit with the sick family member. The sights, smells, and sounds of the hospital room were a little bit unnerving, so I stood off to the side and out of the way as much as I could. For a variety of reasons, my father was exceptional at giving comfort to those who needed it. He was outgoing, funny, and personable. He could connect with the hearts of people in a matter of minutes, and sometimes it seemed like mere seconds. On this particular afternoon, he once again did a phenomenal job of bringing some level of comfort and peace to the patient and their family. I actually remember thinking as I watched, *Wow! He's really good at this! I don't think I could ever do that.* As we left the room, we both shook hands with all the family members and told them we would be praying for them. And they all very sincerely and graciously expressed their thanks to us for coming.

As I walked out of that hospital room, two concepts began to develop in my mind. First, with so many hurting and needy people all around me, I simply had to help. There was no option. I'm not sure what triggered it that day because I had been in hospitals before. I had been to funerals before. I had spent plenty of time in some of the most poverty-stricken areas in our city. So it wasn't that I wasn't aware of the hurt and the need. But for whatever reason, on that day, I could no longer ignore it.

Secondly, I began to see for the first time that I didn't have to be a pastor, social worker, or doctor to have impact. I could work within my natural propensities, skillsets, and passion for business and have just as much impact as my pastor father or my friend's social worker mom or the doctors and nurses I knew. Again, I'm not sure what there was about that day that triggered it, but for the first time in my life, I began to get a glimpse of the road that would be my *journey to impact.*

Initially it was a pretty simple concept in my mind. I thought I would simply work really hard and build wealth by moving up the proverbial ladder of a Fortune 500 company. I would set my financial finish line so I wouldn't spend too much and give a lot of money to charity. I would also spend a couple of weeks each year serving the poor and needy both locally and around the world. But, as you will see over the next few chapters, the journey evolved to become much, much more than that!

The second event occurred about twenty years later in 2011. My journey now involved a beautiful and caring wife as well as two little girls. It included my own impact planning and impact investment company. And, without getting into the details, the experiences and education related to marriage, parenting, owning a business, and working in the investment industry all became important parts of the journey that led my wife and me to begin working with at-risk children in Ethiopia.

My first trip to Ethiopia was in 2010. My heart was immediately captured by the plight of so many beautiful children with so much potential trapped on the streets of Addis Ababa, the capital city of Ethiopia. Africa was on the tail end of the devastation of the HIV-AIDs pandemic, and it was estimated at the time that there were as many as 4.5M orphans in Ethiopia. Most connected either directly or indirectly to HIV-AIDs. As the faces of those children became seared into my heart and mind, my wife, Liz, and I began to think about how we could do something. Anything! The more we thought about it, the more we thought that not only should we help but we *must* help.

Initially we thought we would help with our money, our spheres of influence, and our great wisdom. (Unfortunately, at the time we really thought we knew a lot about how to help!) The more we thought about it, the more we dreamed of funding great clean-water projects and orphan homes for the children on the streets and raising millions of dollars to fund the transformation of all of Ethiopia.

But over the next year, the realities of the Great Recession and its effect on the funding of charities began to set in. Western development dollars, both public and private, dried up. Non-governmental organizations (NGOs) were shuttered, not just across the continent of Africa but across the globe. And the plight of those in need around the world grew more desperate. Our dreams and ideas remained just as grandiose, but the idea of long-term sustainability began to raise question marks about our strategies. If impacting the at-risk children of Ethiopia was so dependent on foreign financial aid (and particularly the U.S. dollar), how could we create an impact mechanism that reduced and ultimately eliminated that dependency? Could we build something that was holistic and sustainable while celebrating Ethiopian people, Ethiopian culture, Ethiopian skills, Ethiopian knowledge, and Ethiopian currency?

As mentioned earlier in the chapter, in 2011 I decided to take a trip back to Ethiopia. My good friend John, who was wrestling with many of the same issues related to impact, joined me. On this particular trip we took a team of medical and dental professionals to try to help the at-risk children of Addis Ababa with medical and dental care. While the medical and dental team cared for over nine hundred at-risk children and their families, John and I began to investigate potential business opportunities that we might be able to invest in for purposes of employing Ethiopians and funding effective Ethiopian NGOs.

One evening John and I returned to our guest house, and after dinner, I went to the top floor and out on the balcony to enjoy the view and the (not so) fresh air. I remember it being a stunning view. The city of Addis Ababa is about 7,500 feet above sea level, but it's surrounded by the tops of mountains, so it feels like you're in a gigantic bowl. From my vantage point, I had a fantastic view of the entire city. The sparkling lights, the dull roar of a city of more than six million people living in an area about half the size of Dallas, Texas, the sights, the sounds, and the smells were almost entrancing. As I stood there absorbing the sights and smells and sounds, trying to relax after a crazy day in a foreign culture, I began to feel overwhelmed with emotions. At first, I was confused. Where were these emotions coming from?

As the emotions continued to rise, I began to weep uncontrollably. My body shook with sobs. It was as if it had just dawned on me that for all of the beauty of the scene before me, the large majority of the six million people that lived in that city lived in crushing poverty with no hope of escape. An estimated 150,000 children were going to sleep that very night on the street. Many of whom were sniffing glue that they somehow got from bottling companies to trick their bodies into thinking they were warm. Many of whom were being sexually abused that very moment by people from whom they were powerless to escape. Many of whom were enslaved in sweatshops. Many of whom would not survive to adulthood. All of whom were perpetually cold and hungry and without hope.

It was at that moment that I realized that grandiose plans and billions of dollars would not be enough to help those children. Foreign aid and development dollars and presidential commissions were not going to bring hope to the hopeless. Because those things, as good as they are and as well intentioned as they are, are incapable of structural and sustainable change.

I was devastated to realize that all the dreams and plans my wife and I had, however well intentioned, were never going to be enough. So, I wept.

A couple of nights later as I boarded the plane for seventeen long hours from Addis Ababa to Washington, D.C., I continued to think about what I had experienced. It was then that the events of the week began to crystalize in my mind. The western world had poured *trillions* of dollars into the African continent since the end of World War II—

and most of it was pure aid money through NGOs and semi-government organizations like USAID and the United Nations as well as other sovereign government organizations. And in many major categories like poverty, life-expectancy, literacy, and health indicators, little to no progress has been made.[1] (Please know that this is not a criticism of the intentions or compassion of the West, nor is it a criticism of many of the leaders all across Africa. It is, however, a challenge to consider whether or not what we are doing is working.)

At the core, my question was about *impact*. If trillions of dollars or pounds or euros over fifty or sixty years have not moved the needle, is it time to take a step back and ask ourselves if there is a better way?

Please hear me clearly. The *situation* all over the continent of Africa is no different than it is in Europe, Asia, and North America. It's no different in Memphis, Tennessee, the city I was born in, the city I love, and the city I call home. It's no different in Detroit or San Francisco or Boston. It's no different than Brussels or London or Beijing. The *issues* may be different. The *painkiller of choice* may be different. But the root problems—the core challenges—are the same. The question is simply this: If so much money has been spent, why is there so little impact, and why, in many cases, has so much harm been done? That question, without my even realizing it, set the trajectory for the next phase of my *journey to impact.*

Since that plane ride in 2011, I have thought long and hard about impact. And, due in large part to many of my clients and colleagues wrestling with the same question, I began to develop a framework for thinking through the idea of impact. If we have so many resources (human, financial, technological, and research, to name a few), why are we making

1. Dambisa Moyo, *Dead Aid: Why Aid Is Not Working and How There Is a Better Way for Africa* (New York: Farrar, Straus and Giroux, 2009) 24–25, 71.

> *If we have so many resources (human, financial, technological, and research, to name a few), why are we making so little progress in areas that matter most to humanity?*

so little progress in areas that matter most to humanity? And that lack of progress is not only in the developing countries that we see on the evening news; it's all across the United States, Europe, and Asia—in the largest, most advanced, wealthiest countries in the world. How is it possible, for example, that grinding poverty exists in New York City? How is it that thousands of citizens were exposed to dangerously contaminated water in the Flint, Michigan, area for years? How is it that only 6 percent of high school seniors graduating in Memphis, Tennessee, are "college ready"? How is it that thousands of people in the United States cannot receive basic medical care?

I began asking these questions many years ago. And the answers led me to more questions. So, in a real sense, this is a book about questions. While it is likely that what you read in the following chapters will raise at least as many questions as answers, my prayer is that those questions will lead you to a path toward significant, catalytic, and generational impact.

Some of the questions we will consider are:

- With so many resources, why so little progress?

- With so much information, how do I fight paralysis-by-analysis?

- With so much need, what difference can I make?

- How do I get started?

This *journey to impact* is a study of paradoxes. On the one hand, it is more painful than I ever imagined. It's painful because the longer it takes to figure it out, the more the casualties mount up. It's painful because when we get it wrong, it has significant impact on the lives of those who desperately need help. Real lives, with real names and real families and real futures.

On the other hand, it is one of the most inspiring and fulfilling journeys I have taken, or will ever take. Sossina's life has been changed. Berhan's life is changed. And they have changed my life as well. An apple orchard has provided one hundred fifty people a job and a sense of security and purpose in Southern Ethiopia. And my wife and I have had a tiny part in it.

My question for you is simple: Will you join me on the journey? It's a journey that will never end. It's a journey that will have twists and turns. Many times, it will require you to retrace your steps and start again. Know that there will be frustration, failure, and broken hearts. But also know that there will be impact. Profound, life-changing impact. Impact that is unique to you. And impact that only you can bring.

Please join me . . . on a journey that will change your life as well as the world you will one day leave behind.

CHAPTER 2

WHAT IS IMPACT?

Vision is the art of seeing things invisible. (Jonathan Swift)

Yogi Berra said, "If you don't know where you're going, you'll end up somewhere else." And if we're on a *journey to impact*, one of the first steps we need to take is defining *impact*.

Let's start with a dictionary definition of *impact*:

Impact:

-The action of one object coming forcibly into contact with another
-A marked effect or influence[2]

The first part of the definition suggests the idea of an object striking another object with force or power. It doesn't indicate whether or not the object doing the striking is large or small or strong or weak but that the power being generated is significant. A nuclear reaction comes to mind. The second

---

2. *Oxford English Dictionary* online, keyword: *impact*.

part of the definition gives the idea of a significant or "marked" change from how things were prior to the impact compared to after the impact. Impact brings about change. Third, the above definition implies that impact can be good or bad, intended or unintended, direct or indirect.

As a working definition for the purposes of this book, we'll define impact as . . .

> The action(s) of a person or group of persons coming forcibly into contact with a need or issue, resulting in a marked, positive change for the good of society.

This definition is not meant to be specific; it is intentionally broad. But it is important because it gives us a common foundation from which we can begin to build our own unique framework of impact. It is the lens through which we will discover and clarify our unique description of impact. It will guide us as we design and execute our impact strategy and develop our impact metrics. And finally, it will give direction through the often tedious process of reviewing and adapting along the journey.

As the process of building your unique framework of impact begins, there are some important principles to keep in mind:

- Your description of impact is *unique* to you.
- The possibilities for impact are *infinite* in scope.
- Impact requires *faith*.

YOUR IMPACT IS UNIQUE TO YOU

One of the great challenges to even using the word *impact* is that for most people, it creates feelings of inadequacy. Martin Luther King, Jr. can have impact—not me! General Eisenhower, the leader of the great D-Day invasion in World

War II, can have impact—but not me! Mother Teresa can have impact—but not me!

I want to challenge you to break away from such a limited paradigm of impact. Because your impact is not Martin Luther King, Jr.'s impact. It's not the impact that General Eisenhower had. It's not the impact that Mother Teresa had. And it's likely not supposed to be! Your impact is unique to you. It's unique to your place in history, your set of skills, your life experiences. No one else has the same unique set of circumstances or passions that you have. And it is incumbent on you to be a good steward of what you've been given.

> *Your impact is unique to you. It's unique to your place in history, your set of skills, your life experiences.*

So start by asking yourself some questions. Below is a list to get you started. But don't limit yourself to this list. Think! Dream!

- What is it that I really want to do?
- What is it that I get passionate about?
- What makes me angry?
- What makes me happy?
- What do I constantly read about?
- What do I do in my spare time?
- What do I think about when I'm trying to go to sleep?
- What gives me a sense of fulfillment?
- What experiences have I had that opened my eyes to a need or an issue or an area of potential impact?
- What brings me a sense of overwhelming joy when I do it?

Are there some topics or issues that interest you or concern you? Again, don't be limited by the list below. It's simply a tool to get you started!

- Poverty Alleviation
- Refugee Crisis
- Healthcare
- Clean Water
- Opioid Crisis
- Visual Arts
- Performing Arts
- Human Trafficking
- Athletics

For purposes of describing your unique area of impact, it doesn't matter what it is. What matters is that it is *your* passion. And for those among us who want to highjack the meaning of impact for everyone else, stand down! You know of whom I speak—people who separate all activities into "virtuous" or "pointless." "Productive" or "wasteful." "Right" or "wrong." *Poverty alleviation is noble. Funding the opera is frivolous. Child cancer research is all that matters. Coaching little league baseball is a waste of time.* If you hear nothing else, please hear me say that I reject that outlook. And I challenge you to do the same!

Do you really think that the children at St. Jude's Children's Research Hospital don't *need* a night at the Orpheum Theater in my hometown of Memphis, Tennessee, while they are battling cancer? We intuitively know that's not true. And research indicates that the spiritual and emotional health of a person is clearly connected to physical healing. But how can those children get a respite without hundreds of volunteers and millions of dollars that are needed to make the Orpheum Theater work?

Do you think that my friends who spend hours of their time and thousands of their dollars riding horses are not contributing to research on how the relationship and connection between someone with autism and their horse helps them cope with their condition, and in many cases, recover from it? Of course they are! Whether they know it or not. And do you think that someone who supports the visual arts *simply because it is beautiful* is not contributing to our world? Of course they are!

> *No one can tell you what your unique description of impact is. And no one can tell you what it is not!*

As you can tell, this is a topic that is important to me. And that's because allowing others to dictate your description of impact or the significance of your impact can be debilitating. It can create a sense of helplessness, self-doubt, and paralysis that not only limits your impact but may, in extreme cases, negate it all together. No one can tell you what your unique description of impact is. And no one can tell you what it is not! They can guide you. They can question you. They can even constructively criticize you. But only you can make the final decision.

YOUR IMPACT IS INFINITE IN SCOPE

One of the reasons defining your unique framework of impact is so difficult is that it is seemingly infinite in scope. And not only is the potential definition infinite in scope, so are the strategies, tactics, and metrics. But the difficulty is one reason we must commit to the challenging process of constructing our unique framework for impact. If we don't, we'll be constantly distracted and wondering if we're doing the right thing. And equally as important, our impact will likely be diluted.

We are not yet to the point that I want you to begin writing down your unique description of impact. At this stage I primarily want to give you the freedom to dream, big or small, and not be constrained by others.

For purposes of illustration, let's consider at-risk children. It seems like a very simple impact target. And it is. I would suggest to you that your "impact mission statement" should be succinct and simple. Just like your company's mission statement or your personal mission statement. But the scope can be overwhelming. For example, will we focus on local, domestic, or international at-risk children? Or should we have a diversified "portfolio" of all of those options? Will I focus on funding, awareness, education, infrastructure, or placement? Am I confident that current research has indicated the best ways to have impact? Or do I feel that more research in a specific area needs to be done? Do I need more training in the field, or should I hire an experienced expert? I would suggest to you that more focused is generally better, but that is a decision you must make. I would just encourage you not to make it lightly and to take your time deciding.

> *I want to clearly reject the idea that impact is separated into the noble or the frivolous.*

As mentioned previously, there are people that would like to highjack your personal description of impact. And again, I want to clearly reject the idea that impact is separated into the noble or the frivolous. In my experience, it's usually the visual and performing arts that get lumped into this category. So let's consider the seemingly infinite scope of possibilities for impact within the visual arts. Will you focus on a specific genre (abstract art, photography, sculptures, etc.)? Are you more interested in expanding the reach of the visual arts for people to appreciate? Or are you more passionate about expanding the opportunities for artists to grow in their work and reach? Is art appreciation among the poor important? Or would you rather seek out aspiring and talented artists who can't afford advanced training and provide it to them? Again, I don't know what it might be, but I can promise you that the challenge will be narrowing down the almost limitless opportunities to the manageable few (or one!) on which you can focus.

One reason impact seems infinite in scope is that impact is incremental. That is, impact is typically created by hundreds and thousands of tiny incremental impacts. And it seems to me that many of the tiny incremental impacts can lead off into a myriad of other paths and experiments! It's like looking at the back of a large antique rug. The back looks like an unruly mess of tangles and snags. But when you flip it over, the front is a masterpiece.

Think of any great impact that comes to your mind. Do you think for one minute that one person or one event or one breakthrough created the impact? Absolutely not! They were all building on the foundation of those who had gone before them. Typically, it was driven by multiple people with hundreds if not thousands of tiny incremental successes and failures across a relatively long period of time that led to the "major" impact or breakthrough.

Another thing I've noticed about incremental impact is that much of the impact was not originally intended to impact the area in which it ultimately does/did. We usually think of the law of unintended consequences as a negative principle. But it can also be positive. How many incremental impacts were unintended? Of course, we'll never know fully, but where would we be without penicillin and pacemakers, both of which were accidental discoveries? And both of which would have initially been considered a failure for their intended purpose.[3]

---

3. Dr. Howard Markel, "The Real Story Behind Penicillin," *PBS News Hour* (September 28, 2013).

Dr. Alexander Fleming is generally credited with discovering penicillin—one of the great, catalytic discoveries up to that point in human history. He stumbled upon the discovery upon returning to his messy lab bench after a summer vacation! Here's Dr. Fleming's take on the discovery: "One sometimes finds what one is not looking for. When I woke up just after dawn on September 28, 1928, I certainly didn't plan to revolutionize all of medicine by discovering the world's first antibiotic, or bacteria killer. But I guess that was exactly what I did."[4]

However, very little progress was made over the next decade. It took years of experimentation to isolate the active ingredient, figure out which germs it was effective against, test it, and so on. One of the key figures in the story is Dr. Howard Florey. Dr. Florey was not only a good physician and researcher but also a master at raising money and handling the administration of the work. He conducted the first clinical trials based on Dr. Fleming's work and, just as importantly, received a grant from the Rockefeller Foundation that funded the research. His organizational and administrative skills were critical to the research and development that brought about the mass production of penicillin during World War II.

Another key contributor was Mary Hunt, a lab assistant, who in the summer of 1941, found a cantaloupe at the local market with an interesting looking mold on it. Evidently, part of her job was to scour the supermarkets looking for moldy fruit—a task for which she eventually earned the flattering moniker, Moldy Mary! She brought the now famous cantaloupe to the lab, and it turned out that the interesting looking mold was the fungus Penicillium chrysogenum. This new strain or species yielded two hundred times the amount of penicillin as previous species and was ultimately enhanced to produce one thousand times as much as the first batches from Penicillium

---

4. Markel, "The Real Story Behind Penicillin," 2013.

notatum. Until Ms. Hunt's serendipitous discovery, there was no cost-effective way to produce enough penicillin to have meaningful impact.

So was there impact? In the first five months of 1942, during World War II, 400 million units of pure penicillin were manufactured. By the end of the war in 1945, over 650 billion units per month were being produced. In World War I, the death rate from bacterial pneumonia was 18 percent. In World War II, it fell to less than 1 percent.

So who had impact? Was it Dr. Fleming, who made the discovery because he was apparently in such a hurry to go on vacation that he didn't take the time to wash the dishes on his lab bench? Did Dr. Florey, the master fundraiser and organizational genius, have impact? What about "Moldy Mary," who evidently purchased a cantaloupe at the market because it had an interesting looking mold growing on it? Yes! All three of them had impact. Along with hundreds of other scientists, doctors, lab techs, bookkeepers, production personnel, and even janitors.[5]

Not only does the story of the discovery and development of penicillin illustrate the incremental nature of impact but it also illustrates in a positive way the impact of unintended consequences. And if you think of the seemingly infinite scope of impact, who knows the number of lives saved and the impact of those lives that can be traced back to Dr. Fleming's dirty lab bench in 1928?

IMPACT REQUIRES FAITH

I would like for us to consider the effect of faith on impact. At a very high level, we've talked about the uniqueness and scope of impact. And it's likely starting to dawn on you that you will never be aware of most of the impact you will have over the course of your *journey to impact*. That's why

---

5. Markel, "The Real Story Behind Penicillin," 2013.

faith is one of the foundational principles of this journey. Because if you don't truly believe that all your energy, effort, time, and resources may one day have an impact, you'll likely give up and quit or at least scale back your efforts. I know I certainly struggled with it.

So what is faith in the context of impact? At the risk of over-simplifying, we'll use one of the definitions from the *Merriam-Webster Dictionary:*

> *Faith:* Firm belief in something for which there is no proof[6]

For most people, *faith* has a religious connotation to it. And I think that's fine. But for the purposes of our conversation, I want to use the definition above along with a couple of additional clarifying words.

> *Faith:* Firm belief in something for which there is little to no tangible or physical proof

> *If most impact occurs by means of multiple incremental steps over a long period of time, it will require faith for you to continue the journey.*

If most impact occurs by means of multiple incremental steps over a long period of time, it will require faith for you to continue the journey. If most impact is rarely seen by the one creating the impact, or at least not seen for a long time, it will require faith for you to believe something is happening for which there is little to no tangible or physical proof that it has occurred or is occurring. If much of your impact is a result of failures and mistakes, it will require faith to believe that your failures and mistakes are building toward marked, positive change for the

6. *Merriam-Webster Dictionary*, keyword: *faith.*

good of society. When everyone around you is telling you that you're crazy, it will take faith to stay the course of action you have chosen.

Impact is interwoven across our culture (both locally and globally). The concept behind the word *culture* suggests the idea of living together in community. And just like any community, most of what is done by any given member of the community will affect others. In many cultures, the sanitation worker is relatively low on the socio-economic ladder. But what happens if the waste and garbage of a city is not collected for a couple of weeks? What happens if the cafeteria workers in the local public school don't come to work? It's pretty challenging for teachers to teach when their students' stomachs are empty! Impact seems similar to sound waves to me. They go on forever, but after the initial impact, we don't usually see what happens.

When you commission a painting from a starving artist, what did you do? Of course, the short answer is that you will never fully know. But it is likely that you contributed to a beautiful work of art that was a part of the heart and soul expression of the artist. And it is likely that you kept their dream alive for a little bit longer. It's also likely that someone, somewhere, will look at that painting and experience a beauty that, even if it's just for a moment, restores their hope or encourages them to press on. We'll never know all of the whats, whys, or hows. But, by faith, we will know that it *is*.

A number of years ago, a friend of mine was carjacked at gunpoint by some teenagers in my hometown. She was a young wife and a soon-to-be mother, so, as you might imagine, it rocked her world. For the next several months, she barely left her home. After a prolonged period of wrestling with her fears and emotions, she began to take steps toward healing. As she slowly re-entered the world of non-profit poverty alleviation organizations, she began the process of overcoming her fears. She began to get more involved with

> *Some people would say she was in the wrong place at the wrong time. She would say it was a catalyst to impact. You can't control your place in history or your life experiences. But you can control what you do with them.*

organizations that worked with at-risk youth. As she learned more about their challenges, she was invited to serve on the board of a local impact organization that worked with youth who had multiple felony convictions. Shortly after, she became the chair of the board of directors. Ultimately, her heart was drawn to serve the very teens that shattered her world. With a deep passion and conviction to help these rehabilitated young men and women, she began to build a business that could onboard those who graduated from the programs provided by organizations that worked with at-risk youth. Today, she provides these at-risk youth job training and a career path that would likely have been difficult to impossible for them to obtain anywhere else. But most importantly, she gives these graduates hope.

You will never meet a person who loves these young men and women more than my friend. Some people would say she was in the wrong place at the wrong time. She would say it was a catalyst to impact. You can't control your place in history or your life experiences. But you can control what you do with them.

In the ancient scriptures, Jesus declares, "You will know the truth, and the truth will set you free" (Jn 8:32). At the risk of taking Jesus's words out of context, if you and I can reclaim a more accurate framework and description of impact that is unique to our lives, the "truth" will set us free to have impact!

CHAPTER 3

A FRAMEWORK
FOR IMPACT

*Spectacular results are always the results of unspectacular
preparation. (Unknown)*

I n concert with the working definition of *impact* we
developed in the last chapter, we must also build a
framework for impact. That is, we need a lens through which
we can view impact. Our definition of impact is very broad
and should be appropriate for everyone in the context of
the impact conversation of this book. But the framework
through which you view your impact is unique to you.

In the last chapter we considered what impact *is* and
to some degree what it is *not*. Now it's time to narrow the
focus to your particular area or areas of impact. As we
discussed in the previous chapter, the seemingly infinite
scope of impact is one of the greatest challenges to defining
your unique impact focus. And if you're not careful, the
breadth of opportunity can become paralyzing. That's why

I have found the idea of a flexible framework instead of the concept of a rigid plan to be extremely helpful for creating your unique description of impact. A framework allows you to have flexibility in the details while keeping you on track at the strategic level. It puts guardrails on the impact journey highway to keep you from driving off the road, while at the same time giving you flexibility for the many variables that will constantly be changing.

As we begin this phase of the *journey to impact*, we'll look in some detail at three specific areas:

1. Passion
2. Skill
3. Experience

PASSION

Let's start with passion. By passion, I simply mean, what fires you up? What wakes you up in the morning? What keeps you up at night? What occupies your spare thoughts? What interrupts your thoughts when you're at work or school or play? What interests you? What triggers deep and intense emotions in your heart? Does injustice infuriate you? Do scientific breakthroughs excite you? Does a beautiful painting make your spirit soar? Then I would suggest that those are important areas of impact for your consideration.

For me, injustice is deeply ingrained in my heart and mind. Very few things arouse my passions more deeply than injustice. It can be as simple as someone cutting in line at the local Chick-fil-A or as profound as young women in Mexico City being trafficked to the U.S. for the sex trade on Super Bowl weekend.

But I've also found that my passions have grown to encompass other areas over the years. I was never really passionate about music as a child. But I took a required fine arts class in college, and after being forced to learn some of the nuances of the great works, I began to really enjoy it. I realized that music lifted my soul to places I could never go without it. So even though I'm not a musician and can't fully appreciate all of the work and skill that goes into it, I recognize how it can impact one's soul, and I want to be a part of spreading that impact.

> *Don't discount a passion or area of interest because someone else might think it's ridiculous.*

Over the years, one of the subjects that continued to surface whenever my wife, Liz, and I would talk was at-risk children. But it took us several years to figure out that was one of our core passions. And now it is one of our core focuses of impact. As you think through your passions, don't limit yourself. And especially don't discount a passion or area of interest because someone else might think it's ridiculous.

I have a friend who loves bees. He calls it his hobby (his day job is an OB-GYN), but he knows more about bees than many formally trained apiarists (a fancy word for beekeeper). He gets the call for many of the bee "emergencies" in our part of the country. His face lights up when he talks about bees. You can't get him to be quiet! Would it surprise you that he is not only having impact in the U.S. but also in southern Ethiopia by helping build and maintain bee colonies that are critical to food sources in Northeastern Africa?

Just to get you started, consider some of the following as areas about which you may be passionate:

- Issues and topics related to your career
- Areas in which your children excel or struggle
- Environmental issues

- The visual and performing arts
- Education
- Poverty alleviation
- Issues facing veterans
- Autism
- Illiteracy
- Social injustice
- Human trafficking
- Athletics

SKILL

Next let's consider your skillset. Although giftings and talents are a part of your skillset, I want to differentiate them from *skills*. Skills are learned, and they are honed with practice. They may be enhanced by talent (think of Michael Jordan or Tiger Woods), but skills are learned and acquired through practice. Very few people (including Michael Jordan or Tiger Woods) are very good at what they do primarily because of God-given talent. In every case I can think of, hard work, discipline, and practice were the major drivers behind an expert in a given field or skill.

Many times, a basic level of skill in a given area is developed fairly easily simply because there is a propensity toward that particular skill. As a young child, I was pretty organized. My Legos® were typically neatly stored in boxes. My closet was usually pretty clean. The books on my bookshelves were even alphabetically arranged by author! No one ever told me to do it, I just liked it that way. I was simply bent toward that particular skill. As I grew older, I continued to become more and more organized, and by the time I had my first job out of college, I could juggle a lot of different tasks and responsibilities pretty well. Up until that time, the skill of organization and administration came fairly easily to me. But then my skillset pushed me into areas of greater responsibilities with many more moving parts. At that point, my natural skills and propensities could no longer keep up. I had to put more energy into honing my organizational skills. Getting to the next level of expertise took years of practice.

If we look at a particular skill on a scale of 1–100, with 1 being a low skill level and 100 being an expert, getting from level 1 to, say, level 80, is relatively easy if one has a natural tendency or propensity for that skill. Getting from level 80 to 85 is exponentially harder. Once you get to around level 85, each additional step up involves exponentially more time and energy. That doesn't mean you stop working on your skill or craft at level 80 or 85. But it does mean it takes more intentional and focused practice.

What I have observed, however, is that many times, the more competent a person gets at a particular skill the more enjoyable it becomes for that person. Particularly if it's in an area in which they have natural proclivities. The more enjoyable the skill becomes, the more they do it (or their boss has them do it!)—and the more they practice it, the greater their expertise becomes.

I love looking at paintings . . . but I don't paint. Why? Because I'm terrible at it. And I'm not going to put the time and effort into getting good at it. So I don't do it. I love analyzing businesses. Why? Because I'm good at it. So I do more of it, and as a result, I get even better at doing it. As I began my career in business, I never dreamed that I would be good at analysis, much less enjoy it. But as my job taught me how to analyze a business, I realized I enjoyed it. Because I enjoyed it, I took every opportunity to do it. And the more I did it, the more skilled I became. The more skilled I became, the more I enjoyed it—and so on. The cycle continues to this day! That same cycle is probably one of the main drivers of my *journey to impact* today.

If you are good at numbers, organization, systems, and analysis, maybe you should consider areas of impact that utilize that skillset. If you are good at vision casting and communication, find an organization that needs those skills in an area of impact about which you're passionate. One of the things I've noticed about impact organizations is that many of them are constantly on the edge of financial disaster, and they rarely have a clearly defined vision and strategy. If you can help in those areas, the impact would be exponential. As a matter of fact, I began getting involved with impact organizations simply because I wanted to figure out ways to make them more financially sustainable and to free the visionary founders and subject matter experts to spend their time in the field rather than raising money or doing the administrative work of the organization (notice how my skill of analysis fits in here).

> *I will promise you this: there is no skill or skillset imaginable that is not needed in some impact organization somewhere.*

Here's my point. You have skills. And you have at least one skill, if not several, that is needed by an impact organization somewhere in the world. In a world of so much need, why not work in an area that you are good at and have a natural bent toward? I will promise you this: there is no skill or skillset imaginable that is not needed in some impact organization somewhere. It may take a while to find it. But the need is there.

Skills, as we've defined above, are both learned and acquired through practice. So, for our purposes, a part of the skills discussion is your training. Whether formal or informal, certified (like a medical doctor) or not (what we usually call

48

the school of hard knocks), your training affects your skills. And the more specific your training is and the longer it takes (for example a neuro-surgeon) the more seriously you should consider working within that field.

I have a friend who is a very specialized physician, and we had some serious discussions about him leaving the U.S. to work as a physician in a developing country. Some of the things we discussed were the years of specific training he had been through, the years of specific experience he had acquired, and the specialized equipment on which he had been trained—none of which was available in the country in which he wanted to serve. After months of thinking and praying, he felt like he would have greater impact by continuing his work in the U.S. while maximizing his time off and wealth to grow and impact his passions in underserved areas all around the world.

Relative to your skillset, you should also consider how many other people in the world can do what you do. In the example above, one source indicates that there are fewer than four thousand board-certified neurosurgeons in the U.S. That's roughly half of 1 percent of all physicians in the country.[7] By the way, according to the U.S. government, there are only about four thousand apiarists registered with the USDA! And they are responsible for over three million bee colonies![8] So, from a statistical perspective, they might be even more specialized than a neurosurgeon and in even greater demand! The point is, the more unique your skillset, the more I would encourage you to seek areas of impact that utilize those skills.

---

7. "Ensuring an Adequate Neurosurgical Workforce for the 21st Century," Statement of the American Association of Neurological Surgeons, American Board of Neurological Surgery, Congress of Neurological Surgeons, Society of Neurological Surgeons (December 19, 2012), 2.

8. U.S. Dept. Of Agriculture Recommendations & Actions: USDA02: Eliminate Federal Support For Honey, https://govinfo.library.unt.edu/npr/library/reports/ag02.html.

Let me briefly mention that making money is also a skill. We all know people who have an ability to make money no matter their socio-economic level, their education, or their connections. They just know how to make money! If that's your skillset (in an ethical and honorable manner, I should add), embrace it. Why spend your time going to Africa to do medical clinics for the poor (something you're probably not good at and plenty of other people are) when you can be making money in your sleep and funding people who are gifted at providing medical care for the poor of Africa? I'm not saying that you should never help and serve the poor. But I am saying that you should consider spending as much time as possible in the area in which you are highly skilled.

I think it's also important to consider your psychological and emotional make-up. That's why I'm a big fan of psychological evaluations, personality tests, and the like. Learning how you are psychologically and emotionally designed can have a huge impact on every area of your life. Areas in which a person has strong natural tendencies are typically very difficult to change. But many times, learned traits and tendencies offer opportunities for change and growth. If you are on the extreme introverted end of the introvert-extrovert spectrum, it may not be something that you can change, no matter how many self-help seminars you attend or books you read. And that's fine. You simply need to find a way to work within the framework of how you are designed.

So, if you are more introverted, for example, it's probably not a good fit for you to be in a position that constantly requires you to work a crowd or constantly meet new people (think primary fund-raiser for the charity of your choice). While plenty of introverted people are fantastic at "playing" extroverts for short periods, they typically know their limits. For whatever reason, they've been forced to learn how to work a crowd and meet people. And they've been able to learn how to balance the hard-wired needs related to being on the introverted end of the spectrum with the extrovert-related requirements of their job or social context. But if they get out of balance for long, burnout is inevitable. If you're good at vision-casting and strategic thinking but hate the details of financial management, you probably should not be on the audit committee! If you're an extrovert and you want to do research for six months a year at a remote location in Greenland, proceed with caution! My point is that while you always want to be increasing your skills and stretching your limits, be very careful when trying to force yourself into skills where your psychological and emotional make-up doesn't fit. Play to your strengths whenever possible.

Liz and I quickly learned that we do not have the skillset to work with at-risk children in Ethiopia. The abuse and neglect that they have endured has profoundly impacted them emotionally, physically, and spiritually. And as much as we love them and feel deep compassion for them, we realized that we would likely do more harm than good if we actually worked with them hands-on. I mention this because Liz is an accomplished primary school teacher. She understands children and has years of experience and training to work with them. But not in the specific arena of at-risk children in a totally different culture than our own. And it was hard for her to accept that she couldn't get into the hands-on involvement of loving on and caring for the orphans and street kids of Addis Ababa. But her desire to have positive and lasting impact overrode her desire to have direct hands-on involvement. So we have sought to work in areas of our other strengths like networking, organizational skills, serving on advisory boards, and funding. That in turn has freed the visionaries and subject matter experts to do what they are good at: working directly with at-risk children. Now they have more impact and we have a part in it!

EXPERIENCE

Closely related to skill is experience. For most of us, the practical training of experience is much more of an influence on the level of our skill than any formal training. That goes for CPAs, CFOs, CFPs and MDs, as well as for skilled tradesmen, IT people, apiarists, and parents (I include parents because it's the most challenging experience I've had to date). One of the best things about gaining experience is that it's never wasted if we are paying attention and seeking to learn. I emphasize that point because I meet so many people who think their experiences don't add any value. And worse yet, some people feel as though their experiences have reduced the value they bring to the table.

I know some people that were unable to attend college because they were needed at the family business. So they feel under-qualified educationally. But in every case that I've observed, the informal education of working in the family business was a much better education than they would have received at a traditional college or university. It was as if they were able to have their own custom-built undergraduate degree program and MBA! And they better understand that people without college degrees can many times have just as much or more to offer as those who have them. Maybe an electrician feels like their career choice is not as important as the CEO of a Fortune 500 company. But they both have skills that can be utilized across the globe for impact. And one is not better than another.

I've met people who worked their way through college and didn't have time for much of a social life. As a result, they believe their careers are in some way limited because they don't have the same connections as their friends whom were actively involved in fraternities and sororities during their college years. However, the work ethic and discipline they learned in the process has become one of their most valuable skills. I know countless women who stepped away from careers to spend more time with their children, many of whom feel like they have less to contribute than those who chose to stay in the workforce. But I can think of several ladies who were able to step immediately into major roles in impact organizations as their time became available. And they not only picked up right where they left off, but the relationships they built during their career sabbatical ended up being critical in their new post.

I don't know what your experience has been or what it will be. I don't know what value will come out of those experiences. But I know it's there. And at the risk of repeating myself, if we are willing to learn and seeking to learn, no experience is ever wasted.

Inevitably, I've found that, at some point, an experience you've had will give valuable insight into a decision that needs to be made for impact.

Life experiences have a profound impact on how we view life as well as how we live it. I have

> *If we are willing to learn and seeking to learn, no experience is ever wasted.*

a friend who wanted to go into the non-profit world. After ten years or so, he was let go from his non-profit job and ended up in banking to pay the bills. Parenthetically, banking was the last place in the world he ever thought he would be. But over the years, he's been able to give more of his time to real impact (as opposed to the many administrative duties he had to perform while actually working at the non-profit organization) as well as more money. And he has a unique perspective on how non-profits function as well as their strengths and weaknesses. My friend never thought he could have impact in banking. But now he has more impact than he ever dreamed!

I've heard stories time and again how desired college majors didn't work out, dreamt-of careers have imploded, and skills that have been hated but mastered have all worked out to put people in positions to have more impact than they ever could have imagined. On top of that, they ended up loving it!

Over the years, our strategies in Ethiopia have changed. But my role has stayed the same. I am good at creating a launching pad for a vision, connecting people, seeing potential areas for impact, and creating high-level deals. I am not good at dealing with the details of running an agriculture company with one hundred fifty employees in a foreign culture. I'm not good at negotiating the front-line bureaucratic maze. And every time I stray out of my skillset and into someone else's, chaos ensues!

As a matter of fact, one of the skills that you need to learn and hone over the years that you travel on this *journey to impact* is having a better understanding of what you are not good at and staying away from it. Whenever you can, stay in an area of your strength.

Most of us will end up having the greatest impact in the area in which we have the greatest experience. That doesn't mean if you grew up on a farm, you'll end up in agriculture. Or if you're a doctor that you'll end up only impacting healthcare. What it does mean is that you will use those experiences, including the ones you hated or felt were wasted, in whatever area of impact in which you choose to work.

As we wrap up this section on passion, skill, and experience, it's important to keep both perspective and balance. I believe in utilizing psychological tests, personality tests, and career aptitude tests to give direction. But just because they indicate you should be doing one thing or the other doesn't mean you should force your way into or out of it. Let it come. Embrace the research and discoveries that have come with advances in neuro-science and psychology. But embrace your heart and your "gut" as well. You'll be surprised at how it ends up pointing you down the road to impact.

It has always amazed me how finding one's passion reveals hidden psychological and emotional capacity. I've also seen how giving voice to one's passion unearths skills that a person had no idea they possessed. And keep this in mind: without all different types of passions and skills and experiences, no organization can be completely whole, nor can they have sustainable, needle-moving impact.

> *Where your passion, skill, and experience overlap is likely your impact sweet spot.*

YOUR IMPACT SWEET SPOT

We've discussed passion. We've discussed skill. We've discussed experience. And hopefully you've been thinking about each of those concepts as it relates to you. Now here is the crux of the chapter, and possibly the most important part of the whole book: *where your passion, skill, and experience overlap is likely your impact sweet spot.* And I would go so far as to suggest that this is where your unique description of impact will likely collide with your execution of impact.

There are three stages to the process of developing your unique framework for impact. You will go through each stage in the process multiple times as you hone your unique framework for impact:

1. Brainstorm

2. Feedback

3. Focus

The first stage is the process of brainstorming. When I think of the word *brainstorming*, I always think of the concept of "spit-balling." That is, nothing is off limits. Just throw out ideas and we'll work with the ones that stick. In the same way, you need to get an idea of your passions, skills, and experiences.

- Schedule a minimum of one and a half hours on your calendar for this process.

- Find a place that is a good environment for you to think (my personal favorite place is the beach).

- Begin writing down all of the things about which you are passionate.

- Write down all the skills and skillsets you believe you have.

- Write down as many of your formative experiences that you can think of.

- Repeat this process several times.

- Go through what you've written down and underline, circle, or highlight what you believe are your top five in each area (it's OK if it's not five, just don't let it be more than five at this stage).

- Draw three overlapping circles and title them "passions," "skills," and "experience" (see *Figure 1*).

- Write your top five in each circle.

- Where you think there is overlap, draw a line to the overlapping part of the circle.

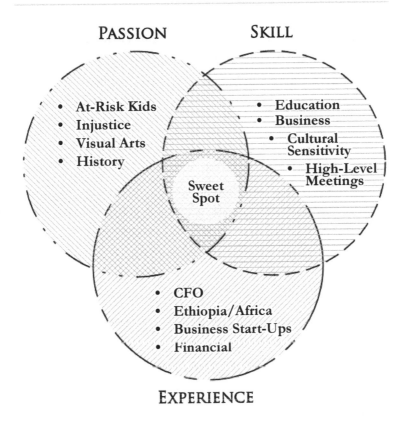

PASSION   SKILL

- At-Risk Kids
- Injustice
- Visual Arts
- History

- Education
- Business
- Cultural Sensitivity
- High-Level Meetings

Sweet Spot

- CFO
- Ethiopia/Africa
- Business Start-Ups
- Financial

EXPERIENCE

Figure 1: Impact Sweet Spot

The next stage is feedback. This is the stage where you will get feedback on the brainstorming stage from a few trusted loved ones, friends, and colleagues. I would recommend three but no more than five at this stage. Briefly explain what you are doing and ask them if you can schedule an hour or so with them to get their thoughts. We all have blind spots, and this is a great opportunity to get an outside perspective. You may think you have some passions, skills, or experiences that really aren't there. You may have some passions, skills, or experiences that you have overlooked or simply don't see in yourself. Give your loved ones, friends, and colleagues the freedom to be honest. Don't defend yourself. Just listen and, if it's necessary, ask clarifying questions.

- Ask your loved one, friend, or colleague to read over your notes from the brainstorming stage.

- Ask them to write down any additional passions, skills, or experiences that they think are important but that you have not listed.

- Ask them to write down any passions, skills, or experiences that are in your notes that they think are inaccurate or should not be there.

- Ask them to draw the three overlapping circles and write what they believe are your top five passions, skills, and experiences in each circle.

- Ask them to give you their perspective on where they see overlap.

The final stage is focusing. Some friends of ours have a beautiful lake house in the eastern part of Tennessee. The house is designed so that stunning views of the lake are visible through walls of windows and a huge deck that runs the length of the house. Directly across the inlet where the house sits is a huge, old tree that is the home of a beautiful bald eagle. By one of the windows with a direct view of the huge old tree, our friends have set up a tripod with a pair of binoculars as an observation point. And every morning when we visit, I always go to the binoculars to look for the eagle. This stage of focusing reminds me of focusing those binoculars to get a clear view of the bald eagle. At first it's really hazy. Then forms begin to be more recognizable. The tree begins to look like a tree. The eagle's nest begins to look like an eagle's nest. As the binoculars focus even more, there are two circles that begin to intersect. When the binoculars are finally in focus, the two circles have become one clear picture.

Again, schedule an hour or two in a place that is conducive to thinking. Then ask yourself a few questions:

- Of the areas of passion written in the corresponding circle, which one seems to have the strongest connection to what you feel are your strongest skills and experiences?

- How do each of your top five skills and experiences relate to each of your top five passions?

- What direct impact connections do you already have that are related to the passions, skills, and experiences in the three circles?

- What indirect impact connections do you already have that are related to the passions, skills, and experiences in the three circles?

- Are you already working within an area related to the passions, skills, and experiences in the three circles?

Brainstorming and feedback are the two individual lenses of the binoculars that will ultimately merge into one clear picture of impact. The more often you revisit each stage, the tighter and more clearly focused the picture becomes.

Ted Williams—in my view the greatest hitter in the history of baseball—was a student of hitting. He created a chart that tracked every pitch to a given quadrant of the strike zone. It was approximately seven baseballs wide and eleven baseballs high. He knew his batting average for every quadrant and, as a result, knew exactly where his favorite pitches were—his "happy zone," he called it. His first rule of hitting was to look for a pitch in the "happy zone" until forced to do otherwise. Relative to impact, my point is this: In baseball, when you have two strikes, you have to swing at the next strike whether it's in your happy zone or not. That's because getting called out on a third strike that you don't even swing at is the worst thing you can do!

On the *journey to impact*, we can wait for a great pitch in our sweet spot, no matter how long it takes. Because there isn't a rule about three strikes and you're out. So be patient! Stay in your sweet spot and wait for a pitch to drive (to use baseball vernacular). At the same time, don't create a sweet spot so small that you never get the exact pitch you want. In the game of impact, in the same sense that you'll never get called out on a third strike if you don't swing, you'll also never strike out for swinging and missing at four pitches. Stay in your "happy zone." Stay in your *impact sweet spot*. Be disciplined. But don't forget to swing!

CHAPTER 4

SIGNS OF
SUCCESS

A good plan today is better than a perfect plan tomorrow.
(General George S. Patton)

O ver the past fifteen years, I have observed quite a few impact organizations as well as individuals who have had significant impact. And it's become a bit of an obsession for me! I hate reinventing the wheel, so whenever I'm around people who are involved in impact, I want to learn from them. What do they do? What is their goal? How do they work? How do they measure success? Are they successful based on those metrics? Does the general public feel like they are successful? All of these questions and many more are fascinating to me. And out of this process of observation driven by curiosity, I've noticed several signs of success. These signs of success are strong indicators of the likelihood of success in a given area of impact.

Just to be clear, these signs of success are present in individuals and family units as well as in organizations. An individual's focus and strategy, for example, may fit on one page or in one paragraph. But it's just as critical as a fifty-page strategic plan for a large impact organization. Whether personally or organizationally, these signs of success allow you to balance passions, financial resources, time, and relationship networks in a way that maximizes impact. They are some of the strongest indicators of success that I've seen over my own personal *journey to impact*.

> *An individual's focus and strategy, for example, may fit on one page or in one paragraph. But it's just as critical as a fifty-page strategic plan for a large impact organization.*

First of all, impact is *strategic.* I have never personally seen significant impact happen without a basic level of strategy and intentionality. Even in the story about the discovery of penicillin in the previous chapter, Dr. Fleming was seeking a cure for Staphylococcus. He wasn't just sitting around his lab waiting for something to happen. Did he expect the discovery of penicillin? Evidently not. But he was actively seeking a cure for viruses. To use the vernacular of this book, he was on the road to impact.

It is highly unlikely that you or anyone else will stumble into impact without a strategy or directional focus. You may stumble into a method or a technique. You may stumble into a sector or focus of impact. You may even stumble into a result that produces impact. But without some level of strategy and planning, it is highly unlikely that you will have significant impact. I would even say that if you're not moving, it's almost impossible to stumble! In other words, if you're not on the road to impact, you likely won't get there!

The old saying that chance favors the prepared mind seems to ring true on the *journey to impact*. I enjoy playing golf. And I have observed that the more I practice my putting, the more often I get lucky. Gary Player, the great hall of fame golfer from South Africa, puts it this way: "The more you practice, the luckier you get." If you are being intentional about what you are trying to do and the direction you are headed, you may not end up exactly where you thought you would, but it will likely be in the general vicinity.

We quoted the great philosopher Yogi Berra earlier in this book. And it's worth repeating: "If you don't know where you're going, you'll end up somewhere else." We started this process with a definition of impact. Your unique description of impact is where you are going. Strategy is the flight plan—it's how you are going to get there. At the risk of sounding overly simplistic, simply writing down and communicating a strategy and then reviewing it periodically forces you to challenge assumptions, make adjustments, and measure impact. I've noticed that one of the differentiators between success and mediocrity is not the brilliance or the complexity of the strategy but simply that there is one and that it is followed like one would follow a map on a road trip.

At a practical level, one of the most needed functions in impact organizations today is strategic planning. In my experience, the typical founder of an organization is pretty good at describing impact. They know what they are passionate about. They know where the needs are. They see areas where they can help. But they are many times not

> *One of the differentiators between success and mediocrity is not the brilliance or the complexity of the strategy but simply that there is one and that it is followed like one would follow a map on a road trip.*

very good at creating and executing a strategic plan because they get bogged down in the details. And yet there are many people (particularly in the world of business) who are very skilled at that very thing. And for the most part, they are sitting on the sidelines. Coming alongside the visionary founder and helping them craft strategies to execute their vision is powerful!

Before we move on to the next sign of success, it's important to mention what I call "strategic flexibility." No matter how much planning, research, and wise counsel goes into your impact strategy, there is only one guarantee. It won't go exactly as planned! Hopefully it will be close. Most likely it will be somewhere in the ballpark. But if you don't plan in strategic flexibility, you are by default planning for frustration and likely failure!

One of the things that I hope you have picked up on throughout this book is the implied power of *focus*. The overlapping circles we discussed in the previous chapter are hopefully a visual cue that focus is a result of this process. Even the idea of impact, relative to its formal definition, suggests being driven by focus.

Out of curiosity, I looked up the definition of *focus*. Merriam-Webster defines focus as . . .

-a center of activity, attraction, or attention

-a point of concentration

-directed attention

-adjustment for distinct vision; also: the area that may be seen distinctly or resolved into a clear image[9]

From that I take that not only is there a center point of concentration but it is clear and distinct. And just as important,

---

9. *Merriam-Webster Dictionary*, keyword: *focus*.

it is implied that when things wander from the center point of concentration or lose their clarity and distinctiveness, focus re-centers, re-directs, re-concentrates and re-clarifies.

One look at our calendars, whether it's on a hand-held device or your refrigerator, reminds us how difficult it is to focus. We may say family is important, but between work, school, and extra-curricular activities, the only time we see our spouse or children is in the car on the way to the next appointment or soccer practice. We may say that education is important, but we haven't read a new book in two years. We may say that at-risk children is the focal point of our impact, but our time and resources are spread thinly over twenty different and unrelated philanthropic strategies. Why is that? We've already talked about the primary problem, and that is not having a plan or strategy. And one of the greatest benefits of a strategy is that it forces you to focus. The old adage that the good is the enemy of the best often seems to rear its ugly head here. There are so many good things available to us, great options for us to choose, that we often forgo what's best and what has the greatest impact. This is particularly challenging in the area of philanthropic opportunities and impact strategies.

I rarely hear of an idea for impact that doesn't stir my heart. And even within our own sphere of focus on at-risk children there are myriad options that we could choose. Several years ago, I was feeling a great deal of stress along with a great deal of unrest that we were not really maximizing the impact that we had envisioned. So I asked Liz if we could spend some time talking about it.

First we discussed how we were spending our time. It turned out we were on seven or eight non-profit boards and traveling two to three weeks each year to learn about or consult on several different impact strategies, and I was meeting on average twice each week with non-profit leaders and impact investors (very few of which were in our area of focus). All of this on top of running a company and spending time with my wife and three small children (can you guess who got pushed out of the calendar?!). Then we looked at our giving. Instead of focusing our giving on the non-profits that we were passionate about and that were in our area of focus and that were having significant impact, we had given to over twenty different organizations. It's not that they were bad, because none of them were. But they significantly diluted our giving to the organizations that we were passionate about and that were having catalytic impact.

> *Focused minds, focused finances, and focused organizations simply have more impact than those that are not focused.*

None of this happened overnight. It was the result of three or four years of drifting where the good became the enemy of the best. We had lost focus. By the way, as this drift happened, Liz and I never discussed it with each other. I say that because your spouse and loved ones many times are the best people to keep you focused. And it's reciprocal, because you do the same for them.

Do you remember as a child, when you learned the power of a magnifying glass? I'm not sure who the first educator or parent was that thought it would be wise to show little boys how a relatively common and harmless school supply could catch stuff on fire, but I suspect they had a little more impact than they expected! How is it that my little magnifying glass could make a burn mark on my brother's leg? (He was asleep, so it didn't hurt!) How is it that something that costs less than two dollars could wreak such havoc on an ant colony? How is it that I could catch my yard on fire with just a piece of glass? In one word: *focus*. A window pane is fine for letting in light, but it will never start a fire. The difference between window panes and magnifying glasses is how they focus the energy of the sun. Focused minds, focused finances, and focused organizations simply have more impact than those that are not focused.

Another important sign of success I've seen across organizations and across sectors is *measurability*. And this is particularly true if you want to have impact. If you don't know what you are measuring, how can you know if you're having impact or not? In the not-for-profit world it is easy to fall into measuring things like donations received or dollars spent because they are simple metrics. But are they really helpful? Building and refining accurate metrics is one of the most challenging things you will ever do. It's hard because it requires humility when you realize you've been tracking the wrong metric or using the wrong assumptions. It requires flexibility because you must make changes based on what you learn from the metrics you are tracking. And it requires courage to make metric-driven changes when they fly in the face of conventional wisdom.

Slingshot Memphis is a non-profit committed to changing the way we look at and measure impact.[10] They have modeled themselves in large part after New York City's Robin Hood organization. The basic premise is to apply the principles of investment analysis to impact organizations. They combine both quantitative and qualitative analysis to identify, fund, and accelerate the organizations that are having true, catalytic, and sustainable impact. They spend the bulk of their energy collecting and analyzing data from a small group of impact organizations and then helping those organizations make strategic decisions based on their findings. For example, if an organization thinks that reducing poverty in a given area is driven by providing job training and job interviews for the unemployed, it would make sense that the number of job interviews would be an appropriate metric. But if, after reviewing the data and interviewing

---

10. http://www.slingshotmemphis.org/

participants and HR departments, we learn that very few of the job applicants know how to interview (i.e., how to carry themselves, appropriate dress, how to respond to basic interview questions), maybe job interview prep should be a part of the process. But how would you know unless you did the research?

It's also worth mentioning that solid metrics are not the end goal. Elliot Eisner said, "Not everything that is important is measurable and not everything that is measurable is important."[11] However, metrics can be a powerful tool. The goal is to use solid metrics to gain insight that will drive catalytic impact in a given sector. And it is clearly implied that when allocating scarce resources, the impact organizations that are having greater impact based on well-designed and well-thought-out metrics should receive the greater allocation of resources.

Another sign of success is *sustainability*. The idea of sustainability has become somewhat of a fad in recent years. So it's worth attempting to define for our purposes. Sustainability has two characteristics:

1. It has the ability to be maintained or grown (both its impact and financial foundation).

2. It "does no harm" to the stakeholders (environment, people, economy, etc.).

There are very few areas of impact that don't have long-term needs. So planning for sustainability seems obvious. But over the years I've seen the devastating effects of people and organizations having initial success and then pulling out due to unsustainability. Many times it's beyond their control. But often it's simply a function of failing to plan for sustainability.

---

11.   Elliot   Eisner,   https://www.goodreads.com/author/quotes/414399.Elliot_Eisner.

Did you know that (as of research around ten years ago) pure water wells in Africa had an average lifespan of less than two years? That's crazy! There were plenty of reasons (expensive to maintain, ridiculous requirements by the aid agency that installed the well, lack of buy-in by the local community, lack of education, etc.), but at the end of the day, ridiculous amounts of resources (time, money, energy) were not sustainable.

Imagine if you lived in a remote village in Uganda and an aid group came and dug wells and provided pure water for you and your children? And then a few weeks later they left to go to another village, leaving you with equipment that was expensive to upkeep and no training to use it? And once it breaks down, you and your family are back to contaminated water and all its resulting health issues. What if you start a medical clinic in a poverty stricken area of Rio de Janeiro, and after three years of providing basic medical care for the poor, you don't have sustainable funding and are forced to close it down? What happens to the people you've been serving? In my experience, many people in developing countries (and the poor and underserved of developed nations as well) feel like they are on a yo-yo! Promises from government officials, aid organizations, and others to provide needed benefits come and go like a yo-yo back and forth. And soon they give up hope or turn cynical.

I can only imagine the number of schools, medical clinics, churches, etc. that have been built around the globe that are in shambles within three to five years. Again, the reasons are innumerable, but many times it's simply because no one thought about sustainability. No one can guarantee anything in this world. But it is foolish, and even dangerous in some cases, to give false hope by promising, or even delivering, something that has no chance of sustainable success.

By the way, here's a clue to sustainability: ask the people you are trying to help what they think. Ask them what they need. Ask them how to make it sustainable. If you want to have true sustainability, ask the opinion of those you are trying to help. In my experience, they know much more about the situation than you do.

Another important sign of success is whether or not your strategy is *catalytic*. In chemistry, a catalyst creates a chemical reaction that is much greater than itself without changing its own chemical makeup. It has the idea, similar to impact, of a controlled explosion far greater than the sum of its parts. I would like to posit that in a world with so much need, why would you *not* want to have catalytic impact? It's not good enough to simply have a strategy or to be in a strategic sector. Are you really being a good steward of the passion, skills, experiences, and resources with which you have been entrusted if you simply accept the status quo?

> *Are you really being a good steward of the passion, skills, experiences, and resources with which you have been entrusted if you simply accept the status quo?*

One of my favorite examples of catalytic impact is the Memphis Child Advocacy Center. There are thousands of reported child abuse cases and child sex abuse cases that occur each year all over the world. In addition to the reported cases, we know that statistically, in the United States, less than 20 percent of actual abuse is reported. And I suspect it's much worse in many other countries around the globe. Whether in developed countries or developing countries or in urban, suburban, or rural areas, it is a scourge across our globe. And it is absolutely critical that we help one child at a time. However, if I have limited resources, in this case time and money, and two or more organizations are helping abused children, why would I not support the one that has the track record, the capacity, and the strategy to increase capacity to help thousands of children? In the Memphis area, the organization that does that best is the Memphis Child Advocacy Center. They help thousands of children and families each year, and they continue to grow their impact. They provide counseling, support, advocacy, and protection to victims. They have a multi-disciplinary team of law-enforcement, local authorities, and child protective services to prosecute perpetrators and child predators and to work toward safety and healing for victimized kids. They engage with hundreds of schools, churches, and businesses to educate thousands of people on recognizing and stopping child sex abuse. They have a great balance of seeking justice and providing care for the current victims of abuse while at the same time providing education and pushing legislative changes that will reduce and hopefully eradicate child abuse in the future. In my view, the Memphis Child Advocacy Center is an organization that is bringing about catalytic change in the truest sense of the word.[12]

As you create a personal impact strategy, one for your family, or one for an organization, make sure that the vision and the strategy allow for catalytic impact. Otherwise, keep looking!

Dr. Brian Fikkert, a professor of economics at Covenant College, authored a book entitled, *When Helping Hurts*.[13] If I was forced to pick just one book impact-minded people should read, it is Dr. Fikkert's. Its premise, over-simplified, is that almost every impact-minded person has pure motives for helping others. They genuinely want to effect positive change, but much of the time they ultimately cause significant negative impact on those they are trying

---

12. Memphiscac.org
13. Steve Corbett and Brian Fikkert, *When Helping Hurts: How to Alleviate Poverty Without Hurting the Poor* (Chicago, IL: Moody Publishers, 2014).

to help. There are many reasons for this phenomenon that are detailed in the book, along with years of research and personal observations, but it reminds me of a phrase often attributed to the Hippocratic Oath in which doctors swear to "do no harm."

As you work through the process of building your impact framework and developing an impact strategy, it is of critical importance that you do no harm! So as you review the signs of success we've discussed above and hone your strategy, you must continually return to this question: Will this cause harm? On the surface, this looks like a simple question. But in practice, it can be very challenging to answer.

Consider a story relayed by Bob Lupton in his book *Toxic Charity*[14] that likely resonates with many of us. During the Christmas season, Bob participated in a local organization's annual Christmas project to provide gifts for the children of families in poverty, as well as the traditional turkey or ham for their Christmas dinner. After some years, he noticed that there were never any men in the homes when the gifts were delivered. After some probing and investigating, it turns out that in the attempt to help, Bob and his friends were actually emasculating the men of the house by unintentionally highlighting the fact that they were unable to provide Christmas gifts for their children. So they would quietly slip out the back door as the deliveries were made at the front door to avoid the embarrassment and what they felt was a spotlight shining on their failure.

Many of us have experienced exactly what Bob experienced. We've provided Christmas gifts to the children of the poor and underserved in our respective cities. Our motives have been genuine. Our hearts truly want to help. And yet, we have, in many cases, caused significant, albeit

---

14. Robert D. Lupton, *Toxic Charity: How Churches and Charities Hurt Those They Help (And How to Reverse It)* (New York: Harper Collins, 2011).

unintentional, harm. It is important to realize that unintended consequences can be devastating.

It's also worth mentioning that causing unintended consequences for those outside the group you are trying to help also needs to be considered. This happens in poverty alleviation and aid efforts quite frequently. For example, if a group decides to provide free firewood for the villagers in the rural area around an agricultural project in Tajikistan, what will happen to the people who were previously selling firewood to make their living? In the absence of something else for them to do to earn income, they have, unintentionally and probably unknowingly, been robbed of their livelihood.

Another sign of success I've seen in impact organizations is *selflessness*. That is, can you say with conviction, "I don't care who gets the credit for impact"? It's amazing to me how many promising projects fizzle out because of pride. In my experience and observation, those who don't care who gets the credit see more clearly, are more open to the ideas of others, and are not afraid to change courses mid-stream if the original course is bad.

> *Those who don't care who gets the credit see more clearly, are more open to the ideas of others, and are not afraid to change courses mid-stream if the original course is bad.*

One way pride seems to reveal itself in the impact world is through what I call "impact silos" or "impact territorialism." Usually a person or organization is convinced that they have some sort of proprietary process or unique knowledge related to their area of impact. And that usually is manifested by an inability to work with others or other organizations and a closed-mindedness to new ideas or strategies brought to the table by others. Some organizations and people truly do have strategic advantages, but it's rare that organizations and people can't learn from each other and, more importantly, increase their impact by working together.

It's worth mentioning briefly that selfless people also attract other selfless people. And the strength of the group seems to create synergy and catalytic impact. I prefer humble and open people to smart and closed people on my team any day of the week!

I want to briefly discuss the idea of *multi-generational impact*. Part of multi-generational impact we have already discussed relates to the sustainability of the impact. Another aspect of multi-generational impact has to do with the scope of the area of impact. Many areas of impact have a clear end point from the perspective of time. For example, the time frame for rescuing the victims of Hurricane Katrina in New Orleans in 2005 and beginning the process of rebuilding was relatively short. The actual rebuilding process has taken years. But the main idea to consider for purposes of this book relates to passing on the vision and purpose of the founders to the next generation. There probably needs to be an entire book on this subject, but for our purposes, I would like to simplify (and probably over-simplify) some of the major challenges.

First of all, multi-generational impact requires flexibility. Even within our own lifetimes we see seismic shifts in most areas of impact in which we are involved. To return to the illustration of Hurricane Katrina: an organization or family that focuses on disaster recovery has different tools, technology, and knowledge that would make their response much different now than in 2005. Can you imagine how it would look in fifty years? Or one hundred years? That doesn't mean that an impact organization focused on disaster recovery changes their mission or vision over the next one hundred years, but it does mean that they build flexibility into the organization's values and strategic planning process. Secondly, multi-generational impact requires balance. By that I mean, there needs to be enough financial resources to allow for methodical planning and adjustments but not so much that it fosters lethargy and empire building. As noted in an earlier chapter, Confucius taught that "money makes an excellent tool but a terrible master." As it relates to financial resources, in our endeavor to prepare a strong and sustainable financial war chest for the future, we can unintentionally create an inflexible and tyrannical master.

Lastly, multi-generational impact must be in the organization or family DNA. By that I mean it requires a deeply passionate heart to have catalytic impact that is more than simply intellectual. It comes from the soul of a person or the soul of an organization. If the leadership of an impact organization or family sees it simply as a job or an obligation or a way to build personal influence, it will ultimately fail.

Multi-generational success is rare. To prove my point, name ten commercial organizations that have been around for more than one hundred years. I suspect it will take you more than a few minutes to come up with ten names. That doesn't mean they're not around. It simply illustrates how difficult and challenging it is. But that doesn't mean we don't do our best to plan for it. If we don't even attempt the challenge, if we give up just because it's difficult, then it's guaranteed to not happen!

The signs of success we've briefly discussed in this chapter are not comprehensive. And some are more or less critical, depending on the culture and circumstances surrounding your area of impact. But they are at least worth considering as you hone your framework for impact. An impact organization or an individual that is not seriously wrestling with the questions posed in this chapter will greatly diminish their impact.

CHAPTER 5

WARNING SIGNS

Where there's smoke there's fire. (Unknown)

Whenever we take a road trip through the Smoky Mountains, there are always caution signs. Most of them make sense. Some of them, not so much! There are the usual speed limit signs and exit signs, but the caution signs are usually much more interesting. *Slippery When Wet* makes sense when you are on a winding road in the mountains. Or *Slow—4% Decline Ahead* (4% doesn't seem like much until you are doing 70 mph with a bunch of eighteen-wheelers all around you!). But occasionally you see a sign that gives you pause. Like *Beware of Falling Rock*. Or *Bear Crossing*. Or one of my personal favorites, *Runaway Truck Ramp* (I've never personally seen a runaway truck, but it must be terrifying to behold!). My point is that none of these signs indicate that you should stop your journey or turn around and go home. They are simply telling you to pay attention to specific dangers. If you ignore them, the likelihood of an accident increases significantly.

In our last chapter we looked at *eight signs of success* that are strong indicators of successful impact. In this chapter we will look at *seven warning signs* that danger is ahead. All of us will wrestle with most if not all of the warning signs in this chapter. It's how we deal with them that is important. When I see the sign, *Beware of Falling Rock*, I don't immediately slam on my brakes. I do, however, slow down a bit (OK, maybe not that much), I put two hands on the steering wheel, and I am much more alert. On the *journey to impact,* there will be many warning signs. As with a family road trip, they don't mean you should stop the journey and return home. But you do need to slow down, be more aware, and take measures to protect against them.

CAUTION: KNOW-IT-ALL AHEAD

Don't be a know-it-all! No one knows everything. It's simply impossible. But after spending a lot of time planning, researching, and exploring your chosen area of impact, it is easy to fall into the trap of thinking that you know more than you do and that you know more than most other people as well. And you very well may! But no single person or organization knows everything about a given subject. You can always learn from others. You may learn how *not* to do something. You may simply have your theories or tactics confirmed. But it's rare you can't learn something from others.

One of the best measures to protect against being a know-it-all is to constantly ask questions. Especially from the people on the front lines of your area of impact. They know far more than you will ever know about the issue. Never stop trying to understand the nuances. Consistently revisit your assumptions. I've learned that when I feel embarrassed about asking a "dumb" question, it's probably a good one to ask! Coach John Wooden was quoted as saying, "It's what you learn after you know it all that counts." That's wisdom!

MEANDERING LANES AHEAD

Don't stray from your unique description of impact. You may not know it all, but you have spent a lot of time and energy defining what impact is for you. Your tactics will certainly change. Your strategy will change, although much less frequently than your tactics. But your unique description of impact should not. It may, and likely will, experience some tweaks and clarification, but it's who you are at your core. It's in your DNA. It supersedes strategies and tactics. As a matter of fact, it drives strategies and tactics. Stay the course. Your course.

REINVENTING THE WHEEL

Don't reinvent the wheel. It is rare that you have an idea that someone else has not already considered. Whenever possible, track them down and learn from them. I'm amazed at how many smart people there are in our world. Smart, passionate people working on some of the world's greatest issues. The longer I'm on this *journey to impact* the more convinced I am that I have never had an original idea! On the rare occasions that I think I do, I'll eventually read something or meet someone that has already solved the problem—or at least is much further down the road than I am!

The idea of reverse engineering is very familiar to those who work in the sciences, manufacturing, and business. Even if you have a patent for something, it eventually runs out and you know that your competitors will have already built their own (and probably better) version of your product or idea.

So you had better be working on the new, improved product or idea as soon as possible.

In the for-profit world, this has driven a lot of progress (although many times the motives and ethics may be questionable). In the impact universe, most people are more focused on making an impact than on making a lot of money. So they are usually more open to sharing their ideas. When you find an idea or widget or strategy that looks like it might work in your sphere of impact, check it out! Learn about it! Talk to those who created it! Not only will you save countless hours rebuilding essentially the same thing, but you will likely add a tweak or an improvement that will make it more effective.

At the risk of stating the obvious, whenever you can partner with the person or organization that has invented your "wheel," do it! If you don't care who gets the credit, you'll be amazed at how much can get done.

DRIVEN BY FEAR

Researchers tell us that most investment decisions are made out of the emotions of fear or greed. When "investing" in impact, don't be driven by fear. There are a lot of different ways fear can sneak into the equation: Fear of failure. Fear of getting it wrong. Fear of hurting those you are trying to help. Fear of unintended consequences. The list is almost infinite. But fear is never a good place from which to make a good decision. There is a time for caution. There is a time restraint. But fear is never a good master. The quote below is attributed to Nelson Mandela, and it has been a good reminder when fear engulfs me.

> I learned that courage was not the absence of fear, but the triumph over it. The brave man

is not he who does not feel afraid, but he who conquers that fear.

Once you've done the research and spent the time and energy nailing down your area of impact as well as your initial strategies and tactics, take the first step. Trust your heart and conquer your fears, one step at a time.

DRIVEN BY URGENCY

Urgency can be a great motivator. But you can't allow yourself to be driven by the tyranny of the urgent. Most of the time the need is so overwhelming that we either move too quickly without considering all of the things we've discussed in this

> *You can't allow yourself to be driven by the tyranny of the urgent.*

book, or we freeze, become paralyzed, and do nothing. Executing a well-thought-out plan almost always leads to a better outcome than moving too quickly. That doesn't mean you don't move quickly in some cases. But quick actions and adjustments to your plan should only come out of a deep knowledge of the situation. I know that the longer our impact strategies take, the more lives will miss out on the benefits. But I also know that building a strong, sustainable foundation for impact will impact many more lives in the long run.

The tyranny of the urgent can also manifest itself in over-work. Working fifteen-hour days for months and years on end will inevitably lead to burnout. No matter how great the need or how important the cause, destroying your body, emotions, and relationships on the journey defeats the purpose.

DISCOURAGEMENT AHEAD

On the *journey to impact*, you will be discouraged. Don't let discouragement win! There will be a myriad of failures, frustrations, wrong turns, and even dead ends. It could be bureaucratic insanity. Maybe it's an act of God you can't control like weather-related disasters, geo-political upheaval, or cultural clashes. But don't let that stop you. Keep pressing on.

One of the things I would encourage you to do is to keep a journal of the wins and losses. Keep a record of those times when overwhelming difficulties were overcome. Go back and read them during those times of discouragement. It will help you see a glimpse of the impact you're having. It will also give you perspective.

I can't tell you how many times I have wanted to give up. And on several occasions I have literally been on the brink of throwing in the towel. But years ago, after my first major battle with discouragement, I printed a picture of Sosie, one of the children our family helps in Ethiopia. I keep that picture in a place where I know I will see it when I get discouraged. When the discouragement gets overwhelming, I look at that picture and I'm reminded that the stakes are too high to give up.

CAUTION: RICH EXPERT AHEAD

> *Don't confuse money with expertise or knowledge in a given field.*

Don't confuse money with expertise or knowledge in a given field. It has always amazed me that rich people are given the status of experts simply because they are wealthy (or at least perceived as wealthy). I've seen this issue become a problem on two fronts. First, when wealthy donors or investors fund a project or an impact investment, it's easy for them to expect a lot of attention. I've known people who fund an impact project or investment and then magically become an expert on all things related to that project or investment overnight. Let me say it clearly: wealth does not equal expertise! Just because you're rich doesn't mean you know it all.

Some wealthy people expect the leaders of the organization to drop everything when they call and execute their ideas and strategies. They suddenly feel like they know more about what's going on than the leadership and staff on the front line. Don't be that person! Just because someone made a lot of money in real estate development for example, doesn't mean they understand real estate in a foreign country and a foreign culture. And it definitely doesn't mean they are experts in the area of at-risk children or the arts! I'm not saying that wealthy people can't or don't understand a wide variety of issues, but wealth alone does not equal expertise or knowledge. Every wealthy person I know has worked very hard to build and grow their wealth. And it is healthy and good to want to make sure that the impact organizations that are funded work just as hard on what they do. That's simply a responsibility of being a good steward. But, as a wealthy person, if you've done a good job preparing for the *journey to impact* and you invest in an organization, get out of the way and let those on the front lines do what they are good at doing!

The second way I see this issue surface is from the perspective of the impact organization. It's very easy to be intimidated by wealth. Especially if you don't have it, you haven't been around it, and a large part of your job is to ask wealthy people for donations! And it's also easy for wealthy people to be more assertive. Many of them aren't naturally assertive, but they've grown into that role because many people around them expect it. However, if you are the leader of an impact organization, a huge part of your job is to protect the vision and the mission. So be cautious as to how much credibility you give to a large donor before you know their real credentials. You can't allow your organization to be intimidated by seemingly rich know-it-alls. Push back. Many times it will earn respect, and it will bring relief to the wealthy donor and investor in that they aren't expected to take a leadership role. But sometimes you'll need to walk away from a donation or investment to protect the mission. And that's OK!

> *Sometimes you'll need to walk away from a donation or investment to protect the mission. And that's OK!*

As we close this discussion on warning signs, it's worth reiterating what we talked about at the beginning of the chapter. Warning signs don't mean *give up, turn around, and go home!* They mean *be alert, be vigilant, and be prepared for danger!* You ignore them at your peril. Failure to recognize and heed these warning signs will mean inevitable failure.

So at the end of a discussion about warning signs, let me leave you with an encouraging word: *embrace the journey!* Ralph Waldo Emerson is attributed with saying, "Life is a journey, not a destination." The *journey to impact* is one of the most difficult journeys you will ever take. But it is also one of the most rewarding. Don't get so focused on the destination that you don't enjoy the journey! Yes, it's hard. Yes, it's discouraging. Yes, it's challenging. But you'll have victories along the way. You will personally be changed. Most of us will not see a great majority of the impact of our lives. And, at the risk of stating the obvious, the *journey to impact* is mostly *the journey*. So don't forget to enjoy the beauty along the way.

CHAPTER 6

RELENTLESS FORWARD PROGRESS

It's what you learn after you know it all that counts. (Coach John Wooden)[15]

C ontinuous improvement is a concept that became popular in the 1960s, and it's been one of the bedrock principles taught at most business schools since the 1970s. As its name implies, it suggests the idea of constantly, consistently, and continuously seeking to improve a product, process, or service.

As we continue on our *journey to impact*, continual refinement—relentless forward progress, if you will—is critical. As we mentioned in an earlier chapter, we should embrace imperfections; but at the same time, we should not settle for imperfection. We should not settle for mediocrity.

---

15. Legendary coach of the UCLA Bruins.

The point in the previous chapter of embracing imperfection was because it leads us to learn and change in a positive way. I don't mind failure, but I hate failure that doesn't lead to learning!

The most important point I want to make in this chapter, as with many principles in this book, is that continuous improvement is intentional. It won't happen on its own. If you and your organization have a deep and passionate commitment to constantly learning, to continuously improving, then your impact will be significantly greater than if you don't. You don't do it just once or twice. You do it consistently over a long period of time. It must become just as much a part of your DNA as your unique definition and mission of impact.

There are three keys to continuous improvement:

1. Asking questions

2. Listening

3. Taking action

It has been said that if you don't ask the right questions, you'll never get the right answers. If that's true, and I believe it is, then you need to focus on the questions you're asking at least as much as the answers you're seeking. Figuring out the question to ask is one of the most difficult challenges you will face. That means it is hard work. But if it's mission critical, then you have no choice. You must do it. Don't just show up to a meeting without thinking about the questions you will ask. And many times, it means you will need to schedule a second meeting so you can think about what you heard in the first meeting and develop new, more insightful questions!

A good example of asking the right questions is related to the emphasis on providing education for girls in developing countries in Africa, particularly in my adopted country of Ethiopia. We would all agree that basic education is a key strategy to lifting children out of poverty as well as giving them a voice against those who would oppress them. Initially the question had more to do with how the government could force children to go to school via legal mandate. In a culture where structure in the lives of children is not emphasized, mandating school attendance was not very effective. Then the question became about how children could be attracted to school. As better teaching methods were implemented along with a classroom environment more conducive to learning, more progress was made.

Finally, the question became about what was keeping children from coming to school. It turned out that for girls, there was at least one relatively simple answer. Girls in rural areas were missing school because they had little or no access to basic feminine hygiene products. It's not that they didn't want to go or that they hated the subject matter or that their teachers were terrible. It's that they either could not afford basic hygiene products or that they were simply not available. Research showed that missing an average of four school days per month was the negative catalyst that led to falling behind, which ultimately led to dropping out. An organization that we support, WRAPs (Washable, Reusable, Affordable Pads), provides a basic feminine hygiene kit to girls in Ethiopia, allowing them to attend school. Simply by asking the right question (*what is keeping girls out of school* versus *what will attract them to come to school*), we can better understand one of the key issues preventing the education of girls in Ethiopia.

If asking questions is important, then listening to the answers is equally important. After all, if you get the question right but don't listen to the answer, what good does that do?

I like to think out loud. But one of the problems with that is that many times others think I don't want to hear what they have to say or I don't let them finish a thought. So I have to intentionally focus on listening in critical conversations. For me that means taking notes, restating what I think I've heard, allowing for dead air, and not worrying if someone else jumps in before I do. At the risk of sounding cliché, we have two ears and one mouth. You do the math. I can't tell you how many times I have taken months or years to figure out the answer to a question that, had I been listening to the stakeholders, I would have heard almost from the beginning. I had asked the right question early on, but I failed to listen to the answer, and the stakeholders were forced to repeat themselves until I did!

Once the right question has been asked (or at least the first "right" question in a series of questions), and the right answer has been discovered, it's time to take action. The process of relentless forward progress rarely introduces major changes. Typically there are small, incremental adjustments. But you must take those action steps! Otherwise, all you have is a theory or a hypothesis. The idea of the scientific method is not to prove that you are always right—it's to prove that a theory or hypothesis is accurate or inaccurate and then build upon it (or in the case when it's inaccurate, to rule it out and move on to the next hypothesis). The point is progress. And you can't make progress if new ideas aren't tested.

> *The point is progress. And you can't make progress if new ideas aren't tested.*

The process we will discuss of relentless forward progress is simply a framework to help you get started. You will likely tweak it to make it work for you and your organization. But whatever you do, commit to it. Here are the steps to relentless forward progress, and we will elaborate on each:

1. Get it on your calendar.
2. Revisit whether your passion, experience, and skill have changed.

3. Revisit the signs of success and ask yourself how well you and your organization are doing.

4. Revisit the warning signs.

5. Revisit and evaluate the tactical and technical issues.

The first step in the relentless forward progress process is to get it on your calendar. That doesn't mean you only do it once a year or whenever it's on your calendar. It means that it's important to you, it's mission critical, and it will get done. The things that you put on your calendar force you to get them done. They are in your face. They force you to make a decision. You will have or will build a culture of relentless forward progress. But if, and I should say when, things get crazy, you know that on a periodic basis, your calendar will force you to sit down and think about how you can improve.

Over the course of our discussion about the *journey to impact*, we started with the impact framework. The three areas we looked at were passion, experience, and skill. The second step in the relentless forward progress process is to review whether or not your passion, experience, and skill have changed. I would suggest to you that while your passions may not change much (in some cases they may change significantly), the other two areas are almost impossible *not* to change. Your experience should be deeper and wider, and your skill levels should be increasing. In addition, your resources will have increased, decreased, or shifted. As you take note of these changes, you need to ask yourself if changes need to be made to your strategies or tactics.

After revisiting your passions, skills, and experiences, reexamine your unique impact vision and strategy to make sure you are still going in the right direction. Then make sure that your actions align with your strategic plan. If any corrections or adjustments need to be made, this is a good place to see them. If you're out of alignment at this strategic level, it's almost impossible to be on track with effective impact.

As I mentioned earlier, Liz and I originally thought that we would be able to be more involved in the actual care of at-risk children in Ethiopia. We thought we would be holding babies, wiping snotty noses, playing games, teaching English as a second language, and a host of other hands-on activities. But we learned over the course of a couple of years that we were not equipped to serve at-risk children, particularly in a different culture with different physical, mental, and emotional wounds and scars. But during the process of trying to help, we learned a lot about at-risk children and were able to communicate effectively to raise funds, promote awareness, and recruit those who were trained to effectively serve the children. By simply going through the relentless forward progress process, we were able to make tweaks and adjustments that brought about greater and more sustainable impact.

The third step in the relentless forward progress process is to revisit the signs of success discussed in chapter four, and ask yourself how well you and your organization are doing.

1. *Strategic:* Are you being strategic in your impact? Go back to the three circles of impact and see if you are working within your strengths. Are you executing the strategy that you designed? If so, has anything changed that would make you alter your strategy? After implementing your strategy, ask yourself, *Is it flawed?* Do you need to adjust?

2. *Focused:* Is your impact focused on the areas that you identified as strategic? Or are you wandering in and out of your strategy? Are you focused on areas that are in your impact sweet spot? Or are you drifting? Was your initial focus flawed upon review? Or is your review confirming your focus?

3. *Sustainable:* How is your progress compared to your sustainability metrics? Is it taking more of your resources than you originally planned? Is it taking more of your time than you have to give? If so, burnout is inevitable.

4. *Catalytic:* Is your impact having, or on the path to having, catalytic impact? Is it needle-moving relative to your unique description of impact? With limited resources, do you want to accept the status quo? Are you content with mediocrity? Hopefully not!

5. *Do No Harm:* Is what you are trying to do helping or hurting? Your intentions are no doubt pure, noble, and good. But are there some negative, albeit unintentional, consequences? If so, adjust your strategy and/or tactics.

6. *Selfless:* Can you look back on your journey and see evidence of a growing ego? I suspect everyone struggles with his or her own human tendencies to want praise and acclaim. But do you feel as though it is limiting your impact? This is a very difficult area to judge. And many times it's intangible. But going to a trusted colleague or confidant is a good way to gain insight. It's important to note that on one hand, you don't want to equate determination and focus with pride. But you also don't want to excuse ego and arrogance on the basis of your determination and focus.

> *It's important to note that on one hand, you don't want to equate determination and focus with pride. But you also don't want to excuse ego and arrogance on the basis of your determination and focus.*

7. *Multi-Generational:* This is a challenging area to see clearly—if for no other reason than that we will not likely see the full extent of our impact in our lifetimes. But it's important to at least consider where you stand in regard to multi-generational impact. Do you think that your organization or the people involved with your *journey to impact* fully understand and embrace your values and philosophy of impact? Not necessarily the strategies or tactics but the core values of who you are and what is important to you? The strategies and tactics will inevitably change over time. But the heart of the matter needs to remain constant. If the core values and philosophy of impact are clearly and effectively passed on to subsequent generations of leadership, success is much more likely. If not, organizational drift is inevitable.

Once you've revisited the signs of success, the fourth step is to look for any of the warning signs we discussed.

1. *Know-It-All Ahead:* Are you or is any of your team developing symptoms of a know-it-all? Do you find yourself not listening to the ideas of others? Is it becoming harder for you to embrace criticism? When was the last time you asked thoughtful questions of the people on the front lines of your area of impact? And more importantly, did you truly listen to their answers?

2. *Meandering Lanes Ahead:* As opposed to focusing on your unique framework for impact, are you constantly changing goals and strategies? Is it hard for you to grind through the tedious and monotonous work of learning your sector of impact and growing your skillset?

3. *Reinventing the Wheel:* Do you feel like you rarely learn from the work of others in your field? When was the last time you read a book related to successful impact in your field? When was the last time you attempted to collaborate with one of your colleagues in your field? When was the last time a colleague in your field reached out to you to collaborate on a project or idea?

4. *Driven by Fear:* Do you have a sense of fear or dread that is paralyzing you? Or maybe fear manifests itself by simply accepting the status quo. Do you remember the last time you experienced feelings of overwhelming fear? What did you do? How did you respond? Did you freeze? Or did you work through it?

5. *Driven by Urgency:* Urgency can sometimes be a result of fear. Sometimes it's simply its own danger sign. Are you finding yourself working at a frantic pace to execute your strategies? How long can you reasonably expect to maintain that pace? Do you find that you are short with the people closest to you? Are you being unreasonable with your team? If so, you may be slipping into the trap of being driven by urgency.

6. *Discouragement Ahead:* Do you find yourself wanting to give up? Does it feel like every day is another failure or immoveable obstacle? It's OK! That's normal. That's why it's so important to keep a journal of your successes and failures. When you're overwhelmed with discouragement, all you can see is failure and difficulty. But reading through your journal with black ink on white paper, it seems to bring a sense of perspective. Not that you won't continue to experience failure but that you will have a more accurate perspective that there is hope.

7. *Rich Expert Ahead:* Please don't be the rich expert. It's eerily similar to a know-it-all, just with the added prickliness of pointing out that you're rich (or at least think you are). Do you find yourself feeling like you have to answer every question that people ask you like you're an expert? Is it hard for you to simply say, "I don't know" or "I'm not sure" or "So-and-so knows more about that than I do. Why don't we ask them?" By the way, those are very natural responses as humans. But it's important that you don't let them become habits. A good way to check on how you're doing as the rich expert is to ask a few people who know you well enough to not be impressed by you—people who will tell you the truth whether you like it or not. Listen to them. If you don't, you will significantly diminish your impact.

After you've looked at your impact framework, signs of success, and warning signs, it's time to look at some tactical and technical issues (step five). This is the area where I see the most adjustments along the *journey to impact.* But you can see that they are driven by a review of the more strategic lenses through which you view your impact. After you've been working in your area of impact for a few months to a few years, you will likely see technical areas of improvement that you can make. For example, is a non-profit structure as effective as a for-profit structure? Do you need to be more involved in tactics, or less? Have you met some other like-minded people whose resources may dictate a more aggressive timeline to meet the impact goals? There are a million questions you could ask. The key is to ask them. And the basic principle is driven by how we can do things better in order to have greater impact.

This is where the tools in your toolbox and the knowledge and skill with which you wield them can produce significant benefits. Organizational structure, tax planning, the use of tax beneficial regulations, and honing your impact metrics can be very powerful. But, in my experience, it seems these tools become more effective once you've been in the trenches for a bit.

As we wrap up this chapter on relentless forward progress, I want you to consider three important areas that seem to require the most adaptation on the *journey to impact*.

1. *Culture:* Cultures are constantly changing. But for the most part, it's relatively slow. It is also typically a painful process. Whether in the U.S. or in an international context, failing to be aware of and adjust to cultural shifts can be devastating to your impact. In my observation, more technologically developed cultures seem to change more quickly. The microchip has probably done more to change the culture of the western world more quickly than anything in history. The world has shrunk. We can get anywhere on the planet for the most part in twenty-four to forty-eight hours. We can talk to people on the other side of the globe in real time. Social media allows the world into our lives. Recently (November 2018), the latest, most technologically advanced rover landed on Mars after a 253-day journey. But, ironically, with all of our technology, our culture is in many respects, less connected relationally. We are more fractured as a community, and our cultural norms (dress, respect

Whether in the U.S. or in an international context, failing to be aware of and adjust to cultural shifts can be devastating to your impact.

for elders, common courtesies, etc.) seem to shift almost as quickly as a two-term president.

Without getting into a study on anthropology, you must pay close attention to culture or the strategies and tactics that were effective five years ago (or even five months ago, in some cases) will not work as well, and in some cases, may work against your impact goals. From a positive perspective, you also have the opportunity to change culture in a positive way. Basic human rights, basic health care, and the rule of law are areas of culture that can be positively affected over time with huge impact benefits.

2. *Technology & Research:* Many times technology and additional research show us that our original ideas, hypotheses, and yes, even undisputed facts, were incorrect. And that's a good thing. Why would we want to continue to do things based on incorrect information? But it's also a challenge to be flexible. Technology has allowed research to progress at a much quicker pace. And sometimes it feels like we're being run over on the information superhighway! Because most humans have a tendency toward familiarity bias, we are comfortable with how we've been doing things. Especially if it's been effective in the past. But we must be flexible. We must embrace change. Be humble. Be curious. Things change. New research reveals new findings. Focus on impact, even when it's uncomfortable.

3. *People:* As simple as it may sound, effective impact almost always comes from people. A wise person once told me, "Invest in people, not programs or organizations." And people can be the most malleable, the most influenced, the most emotional, and the most frustrating beings created! And that

makes it challenging. But they are also the most creative, most flexible, most passionate, most determined beings on our planet! And that makes it amazing! Many times, the people with you in the beginning of your *journey to impact* may not be there at the end. And that's not necessarily because they didn't work out or gave up or anything else with a negative connotation. You'll experience some of that. But people's passions change. Their skillsets grow beyond an organization's capacity or mission. Their personal growth takes them to a place where they need to spread their own wings. Or their skillset may become obsolete for the organization. Whatever the reason, be prepared to have people come and go. And make it your mission to help them be in a better position to succeed at what they are called to do when they leave you than when they came.

You will have times when you have conflict with people on your team. And as painful as it seems, you will have to deal with it. Your focus is on impact. And if people around you dilute that focus or distract you and your organization from it, they will need to move on. But I've found that even when it's a messy departure, not only does it free you to focus better on what you're doing but it also frees them to do the same. You'll also be surprised at how often there is another person in the wings ready to take it to the next level. They just didn't have the chance until the change occurred.

Relentless forward progress is a crucial part of the *journey to impact*. It never ends, and it never reaches perfection. But it's a discipline—maybe one of the most difficult disciplines to build. But, if you can make it a part of your impact DNA, your likelihood of achieving significant, catalytic, and generational impact increases significantly.

CHAPTER 7

THE TOOLBOX

Give me six hours to chop down a tree and I will spend the first four sharpening the ax. (Abraham Lincoln)

As you are beginning to see, each chapter in this book builds upon the one before it. And if you skip or minimize any one of them, it's like removing one of the legs of a chair or stool. Your launching pad for impact becomes unstable! For many people, this chapter is the most difficult to work through. Because on its face, it's extremely boring! But trust me when I say this: if you don't take the time to work through this chapter and understand its basic principles, you will likely reduce your impact in a significant way.

Think about a skilled craftsman. It could be an artist, a mechanic, an electrician, or a jeweler. It really doesn't matter what they do. What I want you to think about is how they perform their craft. They all have a relatively small set of tools with which they perform 75 percent of their craft. And if you were to compare their tools to every other craftsman in their field, they are all the same. So what's the difference between Michelangelo and me? What's the difference between my mechanic friend Brian and me? Primarily it's the skill with which they use their basic tools. Skilled craftsmen spend hours honing their craft. And they are extremely skilled with what I'll call "advanced techniques and skills." But the hours and hours they spend perfecting their skills and understanding of their basic tools are what allows them to understand and perfect their advanced techniques and skills.

My wife is a fantastic abstract artist. But much of what she does involves mixing colors, using different mediums and tools to create texture, and understanding the properties of oils and acrylics and how they work in a specific application. All of those things make sense to me. But I don't understand them well enough or practice with them long enough to create beauty. The same is true of your impact. If you don't understand the basic tools in this chapter and consciously try to apply them to your impact strategies, you will never become an impact "craftsman."

First, the caveats and disclaimers!

Before we get into the toolbox, let me start with some disclaimers. (Yes, our attorney friends permeate every area of our society!) I don't know your exact situation, so anything in this chapter (or book, for that matter) must be discussed with and approved by your tax, legal, and financial advisors. The tax and legal environments are constantly evolving, so the tools we'll discuss in this chapter may not even be available by the time you read this. That's why I will try to discuss principles where possible instead of specifics.

Any time one speaks in generalizations, it immediately doesn't apply to most people! Your situation is *unique!* But generalizations help with concepts. However, at the point at which you get down to specifics, you *must* have advice tailored to your *unique* situation.

The principles we will discuss will be primarily from a U.S. point of view. Because many developed country tax and legal principles are somewhat similar, they will hopefully be helpful outside the U.S. But if you are working or living or engaged in impact strategies outside the U.S., you *must* consult your tax, legal, and financial advisors before implementing your impact strategy.

Did I mention you need to discuss anything you want to do with your tax, legal, and financial advisors *before* you do it?

GENEROSITY

As we begin our discussion regarding basic impact tools, I would like to briefly discuss the principle of generosity. As odd as it may sound, I believe that generosity unlocks the impact toolbox. Let me try to explain. I think most of us would agree that generosity is a good and healthy quality that we should seek to apply to our lives. But what is interesting to me in regard to impact strategies is that a spirit of generosity is like a secret key to unlocking and maximizing the impact toolbox—especially as it relates to U.S. tax codes and regulations.

> *A spirit of generosity is like a secret key to unlocking and maximizing the impact toolbox.*

Ancient teachers and philosophers have long taught that generosity is a virtue. An ancient Hebrew proverb says, "One man gives freely, yet gains even more; another withholds unduly, but ends up impoverished." The Apostle Paul quotes Jesus as teaching that "It is more blessed to give than receive" (Acts 20:35). The Buddha teaches, "Giving brings happiness at every stage of its expression." A Hindu proverb says that "They who give have all things; they who withhold have nothing."

In their book, *The Paradox of Generosity*, Christian Smith and Hilary Davidson summarize some of the key findings from a study called the "Science of Generosity Initiative" at the University of Notre Dame. Their research seems to

101

support what many people have believed anecdotally or experientially and have been taught by philosophers and teachers for thousands of years. Below is a quote from *The Paradox of Generosity*. It is lengthy, but I believe it conveys a great deal for us to consider.

> By finding a substantial life purpose in which to believe, generous people set on a directed life quest with a helpful accompanying roadmap. Naming a purpose, even a somewhat vague one, tends to provide people with plans of action. By organizing their lives around some life purpose, generous people avoid aimlessness, and so are more likely to find satisfaction and happiness. Most generous people relate their life's purpose to a call to reach out and care for others. "George Shyer" in TX is typical in this respect. When we asked if he knows what his life purpose might be, without skipping a beat he answers, "other than trying to help people, no." About two-thirds of the generous people we interviewed deem helping and caring for other people to be the mainstay of their life purpose. Sometimes their answers are somewhat vague, such as "To make an impact and help people, to make sure I'm not just being selfish." More often than not, generous people talk about wanting to be happy. "Pamela Choi," for example, a teacher in her mid-thirties, believes that "life is all about being happy." But generous people are also clear that what it takes to be happy is giving to those around them. As Pamela explains, "At the same time, happiness depends on what [you are] giving to your community and other people." Promoting flourishing of others, she explains, promotes her own.[16]

16. Christian Smith and Hilary Davidson, *The Paradox of Generosity* (NY: Oxford University Press, 2014) 204.

So yes, academic research has verified that generous people are more likely to benefit from their generosity than not. But generous people also have the inside track on maximizing the benefits of the U.S. tax code simply because they have a generous spirit.

If a person is generous, they typically approach their financial situation from the perspective of how much they can share instead of how much they can keep. And if gifting appreciated stock means more money can go to an effective non-profit, that's what they do. If they think a socially conscious for-profit company has a greater impact on more people, that is the direction they go.

Several of the tools we will discuss are related to taxes. Although it's not necessary, if you can understand the goals, objectives, and principles behind a tax code or economic incentives or government subsidy, many times you can better and more efficiently fund impact through those very mechanisms.

Tax Benefits of Gifts to IRS-Approved 501c3 Charitable Organizations

The basic charitable income tax deduction is probably one of the foundational principles for maximizing impact from a financial perspective. To give you an idea of how it works, consider that the highest marginal income tax rate in U.S. history was after WWII when it was set at 94 percent (yes, the good ol' capitalistic, free market U.S.A.). Even as recently as 1981, the top tax bracket was 70 percent. Recently it has dropped into a relatively "low" rate in the mid to high 30s. It sits currently at 37 percent for 2019. If the U.S. tax code continues to allow a tax deduction for charitable contributions, that means for every dollar a U.S. taxpayer gives to a qualified 501c3 charity, they receive a tax deduction (with some limitations) based on the marginal tax bracket they are in.

So if you were in the top tax bracket (not taking into account a million other potential variables unique to your situation), and you gave $100,000 to the Memphis Child Advocacy Center, you would receive tax savings of $37,000. Another way to put it is that the strategic impact organization gets $100,000 of cash, and it would only cost you $63,000 out of pocket due to the tax benefits.

One of my friends considers the tax deduction a government match, much like the match in many 401(k) plans. So, in our example above, the government would "match" 37 percent of the $100,000 charitable gift. Yet another way to look at it is that your $100,000 gift to a strategic impact organization would cost you $63,000 after taxes but would produce an exponential dollar amount of impact. It certainly seems as though the spirit of Paul's teaching that "it is more blessed to give than to receive" rings true from a dollar perspective!

Gifts of Appreciated Stock

Gifts of appreciated stock are another powerful and relatively basic impact tool—and maybe one of the most overlooked as well. In principle, any investment gains are assessed as capital gains taxes in the U.S., typically when an asset is sold and the gain is realized. Any time you can gift an appreciated asset, you don't pay the taxes on the gains in the investment *and* you can receive the normal income tax deduction. To help you get the principle in your head, consider the following oversimplified example and related caveats (which boil down to *don't do anything without consulting your tax, legal, and financial advisors!*).

An impact-minded individual in the current top tax bracket of 37 percent—taking into account no other tax, legal, or financial considerations—wants to gift $100,000 of XYZ stock with a cost basis of $60,000 to Advance Memphis.

Instead of gifting cash, which would result in $37,000 of tax savings . . .

($100,000 Gift) x (37% Marginal Tax Rate) = $37,000

. . . they could gift the appreciated stock that would result in $46,520 tax savings:

($100,000 Gift) x (37% Marginal Tax Rate) = **$37,000**

($100,000 XYZ Stock) − ($60,000 XYZ Stock Purchase Price/Cost Basis) = ($40,000 Long-Term Capital Gains) x (23.8% Long-Term Capital Gains Tax) = **$9,520**

In other words:

100,000 x .37 = 37,000

100,000 - 60,000 = 40,000

40,000 x .238 = **9,520**

$37,000 + $9,520 = $46,520 Estimated Tax Benefit

So your cost of funding $100,000 to an impact-minded, catalytic, strategic organization would be $53,480 net of taxes. Or to use my friend's 401(k) terminology, the government "match" would be about 46.5 percent! So a person gifting $100,000 could actually gift $146,520 if they included their tax benefits in their gift! Keep in mind, the greater the gain, the greater the benefit of the long-term capital gains tax savings.

Donor Advised Funds (DAF)

Donor advised funds have been around for quite some time, although their use by the mainstream didn't really take off until the mid-90s. In my opinion, they are one of the most powerful impact tools available today.

In its simplest form, a DAF is an IRS-approved 501(c)(3) charitable organization to which you make a donation into an account that is advised by the donor (you!). The DAF has the right to disregard your recommendation (for instance if you recommend that they make a grant to an organization that is not tax exempt for charitable purposes), but that rarely happens as long as you stay within IRS guidelines.

Current tax codes allow for a tax deduction in the year in which the gift was made to the DAF. But dollars inside the DAF account do not have to be granted to a charity until the advisor (you!) chooses to do so.

This is remarkably helpful for those who receive large bonuses late in the tax year and are unsure of the amount of the bonus or the organizations to which they would like to contribute. They can quickly make the gift to the DAF, then take their time making grant decisions. They get a current year tax deduction, less stress and scrambling around, and time to make a more informed grant decision.

DAFs are also helpful when making multi-year commitments that are based on hitting specific metrics. If the organization receiving the gift doesn't meet its goals, the funds remain in the DAF and retain all the tax benefits, and the money is not wasted on a failed or less effective impact organization.

Another benefit of DAFs is that they can hold many different types of assets: real estate, ownership of privately held companies, collectables, precious metals, and the afore-mentioned highly appreciated stock.

Lastly, a DAF can be a powerful tool for multi-generational impact. We've already discussed the perpetual need in many areas of impact. A DAF can hold impact dollars built around a long-term investing and funding plan that can last in perpetuity.

It is also worth considering a DAF if you make gifts, no matter the size, to more than ten to fifteen different charitable organizations per year. Your CPA/tax advisor will love you because you will only have one tax deduction notice versus ten or fifteen or more. It simplifies your tax records significantly.

The illustration below shows how a donor advised fund works conceptually. Study it for a minute or two and you'll see what a simple and yet powerful tool it can be.

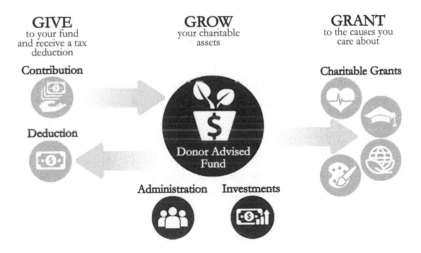

Figure 2: Donor Advised Fund Overview[17]

METRICS

Metrics may seem like an unusual tool for an impact toolbox. And yet we all intuitively know that if we're measuring

---

17. Diagram used by permission by the president of the Donor Advised Fund: http://nbacf.org/donor-advised-funds-offer-flexibility-thoughtful-giving/.

the wrong things, we'll likely get the wrong results. When we talk about metrics, we mean the inputs and outputs which will be used to measure success or failure. How do you know if impact is being made if there are no metrics to track—or if, as we mentioned above, we're measuring the wrong things? I trust that by this point you are at least questioning (and hopefully have rejected outright) that the only way to measure impact is by dollars donated or invested. While that is one metric, it is certainly not the only one, and I would argue that it's probably not even in the top ten for any given impact opportunity. Money is easy to measure, and that's likely why it's one of the first metrics most people look at. But a better lens through which to build metrics is the lens of impact.

One of my favorite examples regarding the importance of metrics is in the area of literacy. Literacy is clearly important, and most would say critical, to getting out of poverty. So it would make sense that funding literacy programs would be a very powerful impact investment. For years, impact in the literacy world simply revolved around how many people an organization could take through a literacy training program after which they would take a test confirming that they could read on a twelfth-grade level. If a program could graduate a few people that could pass the test, they were successful. And the more people you helped pass the test, the more successful the organization.

But more recently, research has shown that the most important level of reading is the second-grade level. Because that is generally when you go from learning to read to reading to learn. That is when your ability to learn takes a quantum leap forward. As a percentage, many more resources are spent on getting people from a second grade reading level to a twelfth grade reading level than are spent on reaching the second-grade level. But the payoff is not nearly as significant. Once a person can read to learn, they now have the tools to take the responsibility to grow and learn themselves. At that point, research suggests that higher payoff programs such as how to successfully navigate the job interview process or job training should receive more resources. But if we are measuring irrelevant or immaterial metrics, how would we know?

There are many resources on this topic, and I would encourage you to read as much as you can. There may already be a metric system that fits your strategy. But you also may need to build your own. It's hard work, but if you don't know what you're measuring, not only are you likely to fail but you are also likely to hurt the very people and organizations you are trying to help. A good place to start is the Robin Hood organization's website.[18]

IMPACT CATALYST ORGANIZATIONS

A more recently developed tool for your toolbox is an organization, typically structured as a non-profit, that focuses on many of the issues we've discussed and who invests their dollars in the non-profits that are creating the most impact. This is a powerful tool for those who may not have the financial resources or time available to put into building their own metrics and detailed impact strategies. The Robin Hood organization mentioned above was one of the early adopters of this type of organizational structure and strategy. They take a very disciplined approach, similar to a for-profit company, and they work to discover which impact organizations are having the best, most catalytic impact for the resources with which they are entrusted. Once they determine the top performers, they make major investments in those organizations and help them scale up their impact. It's a very efficient way for an impact investor to have a high degree of confidence that their resources are being maximized in their area of passion.

---

18. Robinhood.org

IMPACT-MINDED FOR-PROFIT BUSINESSES

Another concept that is growing in popularity is the idea of impact-minded for-profit businesses. If you are impact minded, you simply must be aware of this option on the impact spectrum and at least consider whether or not it may be a fit for your area of impact. There are many different names for these types of organizations (socially responsible, triple-bottom line—financial, social, environmental—social impact investments, venture philanthropy, etc.), but the common denominator is a focus on profit *and* social/environmental benefits. Many people feel that a business should focus on maximizing shareholder profit. And one could make a legal argument that that is true. But practically every business spends money on "soft" issues (local non-profits, extra employee benefits, etc.).

The difference seems to be the motive. For those who focus on profit, the motivation is likely that the "soft" expenses generate financial benefits over the long run (public relations, employee loyalty, customer loyalty, lower employee turn-over, etc.) or that it's simply a cost of doing business. Impact-minded businesses feel that profit and social/environmental impact are not exclusive but mutually inclusive to the operation of the business. Impact-minded businesses typically take a holistic approach to their organizational structure, purpose, and strategic vision. Impact businesses seem, in my experience, to be especially effective in developing countries. While not for everyone, impact-minded for-profit businesses need to be on your radar screen and a part of the consideration process for all of us.

> *Impact-minded businesses feel that profit and social/environmental impact are not exclusive but mutually inclusive to the operation of the business.*

EXPLORATORY TRIPS & VISITS

Many people feel that spending time and money on investigative trips is a waste. But I believe it is one of the single most important practices you can employ. As a matter of fact, I would argue that it is more important than anything else we've discussed in this chapter.

If you want to impact literacy issues for inner-city children in your city, doesn't it seem wise to make several visits to the local literacy center or school program? If you want to impact healthcare in a developing country, don't you think you ought to take a trip or two to that particular country to understand from the stakeholders what the real issues are?

We would never consider a major investment or a major initiative or a major undertaking in any other area of our lives without doing extensive research. And yet in the area of impact, we hardly do any. Visiting the Memphis Child Advocacy Center helped Liz and me better understand what they were doing and how they were doing it. It also gave us a sense, and a feel, that this organization and its people were right for us.

The first couple of trips I took to Ethiopia were centered around medical missions. But I would use a lot of my time there learning about the culture, investigating the political and tax structure of the country, and meeting local business and NGO leaders. After I realized how important it was to explore Ethiopia and its culture, we began to take trips with no other purpose than to learn.

If I had not taken the years to explore Ethiopia, I wouldn't understand the challenge it is to communicate in a country with over eighty different languages and two hundred different dialects. I wouldn't understand the differences between the Orthodox Church, the Evangelical Church, the Muslim community, and the traditional tribal communities—differences that are unique to Ethiopia and influence every nook and cranny of the culture. If I had not

111

taken the time to explore Ethiopia, I wouldn't understand how their banking system works, that they are starved for U.S. dollar reserves, and that they have a curious balance of optimism and skepticism for foreign investment.

My point is that you need to take the time to not only read and research and talk to people in the area in which you want to have impact, but you need to experience it. And that becomes even more critical if it's in a culture that is different from your own.

Just like a skilled tradesperson has specialized tools that are important for the particular specialized trade they work in, you and I, in the impact trade, will accumulate tools that are specialized to our particular area of impact. But every skilled tradesperson has the same basic set of tools. The ones mentioned above are certainly not exhaustive, nor are they particularly specialized. But they are critically important. And they need to be in everyone's toolbox. By simply understanding these basic tools, your impact will be significantly more effective.

As we close this brief look at some basic tools of impact, I want to leave you with a quote attributed to Francis of Assisi:

> He who works with his hands is a laborer. He who works with his hands and his head is a craftsman. He who works with his hands and his head and his heart is an artist.

Just as an artist works with his hands, his head, *and* his heart, those of us who want to have significant, catalytic, and sustainable impact must do the same.

CHAPTER 8

GET OFF THE BENCH

They on the heights are not the souls
Who never erred or went astray,
Or reached those high rewarding goals
Along a smooth, flower-bordered way.
Nay, those who stand where first comes dawn
Are those who stumbled but went on.
(Dr. J. S. Baxter)[19]

Theodore Roosevelt said these words,

It is not the critic who counts; not the man who points out how the strong man stumbles, or where the doer of deeds could have done them better. The credit belongs to the man who is actually in the arena, whose face is marred by dust and sweat and blood; who strives valiantly; who errs,

---

19. J. S. Baxter, *Explore the Book* (Nashville, TN: Zondervan, 1987).

who comes short again and again, because there is no effort without error and shortcoming; but who does actually strive to do the deeds; who knows great enthusiasms, the great devotions; who spends himself in a worthy cause; who at the best knows in the end the triumph of high achievement, and who at the worst, if he fails, at least fails while daring greatly, so that his place shall never be with those cold and timid souls who neither know victory nor defeat.[20]

Up till now, everything in this book has been about preparing for the journey. And, preparation is a vital part of the journey. But now is the time for action! Now it's time to get in the car. It's time to board the airplane. It's time to begin the journey!

I distinctly remember a time this happened to me. After approximately five years of building our unique framework for impact, designing our plan, researching opportunities, and learning about the culture, there was a clear point in time where the decision was made to execute the plan. My friends and colleagues John Ozier and Jonathan Bridges were sitting in the living room at our guest house in Addis Ababa, Ethiopia. We had spent five years specifically planning and seeking out an impact investment in the country of Ethiopia. Jonathan had actually moved to Ethiopia with his family permanently in order to immerse himself in the culture, learn the language, and begin testing and researching different impact ideas. There were trips back and forth between the U.S. and Ethiopia. There were thousands of kilometers driving around Ethiopia looking, learning, exploring, and meeting people. We were deeply invested in what we affectionately referred to as our adopted country. We had spent hundreds, if not thousands of hours building spreadsheets and running

---

20. According to The Teddy Roosevelt Center (theodorerooseveltcenter.org), Theodore Roosevelt said this in a speech in France in 1920.

different scenarios. But as we sat there, we all felt like this was the moment of decision.

I remember there being a long period of silence (I'm sure it was only a few seconds, but it felt like ten minutes). As I thought about what we wanted to do, all of the fears and worries and what-ifs came flooding back into my mind. All of the scenarios that we had run on the spreadsheets that were failures rushed into my mind. And I'll confess, I was overcome with fear. But as I thought about all of the potential dangers and chances of failure, I also began to think of the potential for life-changing impact. Jobs for people that could lift them from devastating poverty and restore dignity to their lives. Children going to school who previously could not. Hope for people who had none. And then I felt a sense of peace and a sense of calling that fought back the fear. The fear wasn't gone, but it no longer overwhelmed me. I remember having an almost out-of-body experience. I could hear myself saying almost exactly what John and Jonathan were simultaneously expressing out loud: *This is it. I believe this is what God wants us to do. Let's do it.*

Franklin D. Roosevelt said, "Courage is not the absence of fear, but rather the assessment that something else is more important than fear of failure." The fears the three of us felt before we said, "Let's do it" didn't go away. But seeing the gravity of the impact and how important it was both in our own lives and in the lives of the people we serve in Ethiopia led us to make the commitment—to jump off the cliff.

As you can see, the decision to execute your impact strategy is not the beginning of the journey. The journey began much earlier simply as an idea or dream or vision. And, as you will likely see years down the road, the decision to execute will be one of several pivotal moments in your *journey to impact*. In a very real sense, executing your impact strategy is just another part of the process. It's the next step on the journey. If you stop at the point of decision or lose your focus, the journey will slow and maybe even stop. Because you never get it perfect. It never goes exactly according to plan. But each attempt to execute your strategy will result in new information to hone it. Every mistake you make is an opportunity to revisit your assumptions and make adjustments.

As you continually revisit your unique description of impact, it will help keep you focused. As you continue to revisit the design of your plan, you will continue refining it. As you continue to measure your impact against the metrics you've developed, you will constantly enhance them. All of these things you've been thinking about will unknowingly become a framework through which, consciously and unconsciously, you continue to refine and enhance and hone over and over and over again your ideas of impact, their execution and their metrics.

> *Being strategic is important. Thoughtful planning is important. Understanding your impact framework is important. But at some point, you have to do it.*

When Liz and I began our *journey to impact*, I'm not sure we really knew we had started. But as our calling and mission began to become clearer, we could look back and see that, without a doubt, the direction was clearly orchestrated to go in a specific direction.

Maybe the whole key to impact is simply getting started. Being strategic is important. Thoughtful planning is important. Understanding your impact framework is important. But at some point, you have to do it. A friend used to tell me, "It's hard to steer a ship at anchor." And that's very true. Once you have your flight plan and you've checked the weather, loaded the plane, and worked through the pre-flight checklist, you've got to take off! And no experienced pilot would ever expect to make it through a long flight without course corrections! It's the same for you. But you'll never get to the destination of impact unless you get started.

If one of the most important keys to impact is getting started, I would also suggest that it is one of the greatest barriers to impact. I think that is because no matter how much time and energy you put into strategy and planning, you *will* experience failures and setbacks. And, speaking from the perspective of a perfectionist, that is frightening. Not because I fear failure so much as I fear hurting other people. If the area of impact that you have chosen is important (and it will be important, or you would not have chosen it), then failures have a human cost to them. And sometimes that cost is significant. But you will somehow need to learn that there is a balance between striving for impact while experiencing failures.

For Liz and me, it came down to a fairly simple equation. The need is overwhelming, so we must do something. If we must do something, then let's do something that will have significant impact. If we are committed to learning from our mistakes and making course corrections as quickly as possible, then we will get closer to impact more quickly the sooner we start. So we plan, we go through the process of relentless forward progress, we pray, and we move forward.

I would like to close with two stories. One story is about someone who "does" the impact. He is hands-on and up close and personal, and he lives to touch the lives in his sphere of influence. The second story is about someone who "funds" the impact. They are not as hands-on or as up close and personal as the first story. But they fund the impact organizations that are. And both are critical to impact. What I hope you will see from these two examples is that impact takes place across a spectrum. And there is a place for you and your unique definition of impact somewhere along that spectrum.

"THE DOER"

In 1999 Steve started an impact organization focused on bringing economic stability to the third poorest zip code in the nation at the time—Advance Memphis. Steve didn't come from money, and he didn't have a lot of wealthy contacts. But he knew he had to do something to help the people that lived in the 38126 zip code of Memphis, Tennessee. Steve started the work by helping friends from the neighborhood connect with job opportunities. As he continued serving and dreaming, staff and programs were added, beginning with financial literacy programs and growing to include job readiness and much more.

Steve knew that it wasn't enough to simply offer a job to someone who had been born and raised in generational poverty. But he wasn't sure exactly how to provide a different type of assistance. So, with plenty of trial and error, financial literacy grew to job skills training, which then grew to job interview training, which then grew to job placement, and so on. Advance Memphis has developed the idea of "stepping stone" programs to help students move toward economic stability. Matched savings programs, GED preparation, an addiction recovery program, and many more "stepping stones" are part of the strategy.

Steve and the team at Advance Memphis epitomize what it means to stay focused on the vision to impact the 38126 zip code. They remain committed to deepening what they call "reciprocal learning relationships" with people they serve as well as with subject experts across the U.S. They are quick to try new ideas and just as quick to move on from failed ones. Has it been a success? It seems as though it has. Today, Advance Memphis has almost doubled the wages earned by their 38126 neighbors that work in their outsourcing operation. Over the past five years, their two warehouse operations have generated around 75 percent of the revenue necessary to run a sustainable impact business without a need for charitable contributions. And they are graduating almost one hundred chronically unemployed individuals each year through their job readiness and soft skills program.

Is it difficult? I can't imagine the level of frustration and discouragement serving those battling addictions. And the more I learn about the effects of generational poverty, I can only imagine how difficult the work of Advance Memphis must be. Will the mission ever be fully accomplished? Probably not in the sense of a 100 percent poverty-free zip code. But certainly in the sense of moving the needle significantly. Steve's vision that turned into Advance Memphis is sustainable, it's catalytic, and it has the ability and capacity to continue to change thousands of lives.

"THE FUNDER"

David came from an impact-minded family. His father was a scientist who worked for years on projects to provide cleaner, safer drinking water for the people of Africa. So the concept of giving back, helping those in need, and the responsibility to leave the world in better shape than how he found it were not foreign to him.

After many years of leading the family business, he went on a trip to Africa to investigate the sustainability of providing pure water for the people of Uganda. During that trip and several subsequent trips, he began to realize that sustainable, catalytic impact in Uganda as well as across the continent of Africa was more than simply exporting Western expertise, knowledge, and methods. It was a much more nuanced and culturally driven mission than he had ever expected.

As he considered his experiences and all that he had learned, he became convinced that his path to impact, his unique description of impact, involved helping young entrepreneurs across the continent of Africa. That involved economics, finance, funding, business analysis, and leadership skills—all of which he had honed over years of running a business in the U.S. There is also a wisdom that comes from years of experience that, many times, is cross-cultural.

So David began to investigate the best ways to help. As fate would have it, he met two young men fresh out of college with a burning passion to save the world. Their goal was to build a socially responsible investment group that would fund and own businesses across Africa. As might be expected of recent graduates, there was a lot of zeal but maybe a little less wisdom! It turned out to be a perfect project for David. He was able to give counsel and guidance, introduce them to other impact-minded investors, provide some seed funding for their project, and ultimately learn as much from the young guys as they learned from him!

Was it successful? I think so. From a social perspective, one of the businesses transformed the poultry industry in East Africa by employing thousands of indigenous employees and sub-contractors, many of whom are women. They've provided a protein-rich food to millions who didn't have access to it before. They've provided small business opportunities for thousands of small-holder farmers. They've provided job skills and business training for hundreds. Financially, they've not only returned the initial investments but actually made a profit (which is very difficult to do in impact investments).

Was is difficult? From my perspective as an outside observer, I would say it was brutal. There were plenty of times when David as well as the senior management team were discouraged, exhausted, and even at the precipice of giving up. But they stayed with it.

Did they learn anything? Absolutely! They learned more in six or seven years than most people learn in a lifetime. And now, that education from the School of Hard Knocks has prepared them for even greater success in their impact ventures to come.

IN CONCLUSION

As I mentioned above, impact is a spectrum. And these two stories demonstrate not only how wide the spectrum is but that anywhere along it is critical. And everyone's unique place on the spectrum is necessary.

When I started working on this book, I believed that significant impact was simply a result of thinking, planning, and executing. In other words, it was intentional. And without intentionality, there could be no impact. After all the research and thinking and writing, I still believe that to be absolutely true. But there is one caveat and that is this: Everyone on this planet will have impact, whether it's intentional or not. The question is, what kind of impact will it be? May I suggest to you that if you are not intentional about your impact, it will at best be tepid. If you fail to go through the process described in this book, you may have impact, but it is not likely to be significant. And at worst, it will cause harm. Unintentional harm to be sure, but harm nonetheless. And maybe even more disturbing, you will have squandered your unique and critical talents, gifts, and resources.

However, if you are intentional about your impact, you are much more likely to have positive, catalytic, and critical impact. You may look back on your impact years later and not see much, but it will be there. History may not look back and see the impact of your life, but it will be there in the lives in whom you have invested. So don't shortcut the process!

This book is intended for people all across the spectrum of impact. If you're new to the *journey*, you may have never even considered that you can be a part of something bigger than yourself. Or maybe you've been thinking about impact but had no idea where to begin. Now is the time to get started! This book and the resources in it are designed to help you build a solid foundation for impact. Use it!

Maybe, after a good start, your *journey* has stalled because you've become overwhelmed or cynical. Or maybe you've simply run out of fuel emotionally, physically, or financially. Now is the time to get back in the game! This book and the resources in it are designed to help you refocus and refuel for impact. Use it!

Maybe you've had a great start that has resulted in great impact. Maybe you've had impact that you never dreamed you would. Now is the time to ask yourself if your impact can be even greater! Now is the time to share what you've learned with the impact community around you. This book and the resources in it are designed to help you create and build on the DNA of continuous improvement. Use it!

My friend, we all have impact. The question is whether or not it's the impact you and I want to have. My prayer is that this book will give you hope that *you* can have impact. That it will give you the freedom to embrace your own unique passions, skills, and life experiences. And that it will give you a practical framework to design and implement impact that is strategic, sustainable, and catalytic. Your *journey to impact* begins with your heart. It develops with your mind. And it results in action.

> *Your journey to impact begins with your heart. It develops with your mind. And it results in action.*

Chapter one ended with a simple question. And it's the same question that will end this chapter as well as this book: Will you join us on the *journey?* It's a *journey* that will never end. It's a *journey* that will have twists and turns. It will require you to, many times, retrace your steps and start again. Know that there will be frustration, failure, and broken hearts. But also know that there will be impact. Profound, life-changing impact. Impact that is unique to you. And impact that only you can bring.

Please join me . . . on a *journey* that will change your life as well as the world you will one day leave behind.

Godspeed.

RESOURCES

BOOKS

Cadbury, Deborah, *Chocolate Wars* (New York: Public Affairs, 2010).

Collins, Jim, *Good to Great and the Social Sectors* (New York: Harper Collins Publishers, 2001).

Corbett, Steven & Brian Fikkert, *When Helping Hurts: How to Alleviate Poverty Without Hurting the Poor* (Chicago, IL: Moody Publishers, 2014).

Evenett, Dr. Rupert & Karl H. Richter, *Making Good in Social Impact Investment* (The City UK: The Social Investment Business, 2011).

Goldsmith, Stephen, *The Power of Social Innovation* (San Francisco, CA: John Wiley and Sons Inc., 2010).

Grennan, Conor, *Little Princes* (New York: Harper Collins Publishers, 2010).

Hancock, Graham, *Lords of Poverty* (New York: Grove/Atlantic, Inc, 1989).

Lingenfelter, Sherwood G., *Leading Cross-Culturally* (Grand Rapids, MI: Baker Publishing Group, 2008).

Lupton, Robert D., *Toxic Charity: How Churches and Charities Hurt Those They Help (And How to Reverse It)* (New York: Harper Collins, 2011).

Maranz, David E., *African Friends and Money Matters* (Dallas, TX: SIL International, 2001).

Minnich, Aimee, *The Profitable Charity* (United States, Aimee Minnich, 2015).

Moyo, Dambisa, *Dead Aid* (New York: Farrar, Straus, and Giroux, 2009).

Payne, Ruby K., *A Framework for Understanding Poverty* (Highlands, TX: Aha! Process Inc., 2005).

Rosling, Hans, Anna Rosling Ronnlund & Ola Rosling, *Factfulness* (New York: Flatiron Books, 2018).

Smith, Christian & Hilary Davidson, *Paradox of Generosity* (New York: Oxford University Press, 2014).

Tierney, Thomas J. & Joel L. Fleishman, *Give Smart* (New York: Public Affairs, 2011).

ONLINE TOOLS & RESOURCES

Impact Foundation – *impactfoundation.org*

The Philanthropic Initiative – *tip.org*

Inspired Philanthropy – *inspiredphilanthropy.org*

Foundation Source – *foundationsource.com*

The Giving Pledge – *givingpledge.org*

Generous Giving – *generousgiving.org*

The Gathering – *Thegathering.com*

The Bridgespan Group – *bridgespan.org*

2164 – *2164.net*

Lucy Bernholz - *Lucybernholz.com*

Planned Giving Design Center – *pgdc.com*

IBEC Ventures – *ibecventures.com*

Charity Navigator - *charitynavigator.org*

Guidestar – *guidestar.com*

Mats Tunehag - *Matstunehag.com*

Praxis Labs - *PraxisLabs.org*

IMPACT ORGANIZATIONS

Memphis Child Advocacy Center – *memphiscac.org*

Advance Memphis – *advancememphis.org*

Slingshot Memphis – *slingshotmemphis.org*

Robin Hood – NYC – *robinhood.org*

Impact Foundation – *impactfoundation.com*

Sweet LaLa's – *sweetlalas.com*

Wakami – *wakimiglobal.com*

Christian Community Foundation – *ccfmemphis.com*

The Community Foundation of Greater Memphis – *cfgm.org*

Highland Harvesters – *highlandharvesters.com*

OTHER RESOURCES

Alimayu Reunited with His Mother Video – youtube.com/
watch?v=mn5BEkEkT1I

The Gillentine Group – www.EdGillentine.com—Please visit
our website for free supplemental material for this book.